MIDLIFE

MIDLIFE

a philosophical Guide

Kieran Setiya

PRINCETON UNIVERSITY PRESS
PRINCETON AND OXFORD

Published by Princeton University Press,
41 William Street, Princeton, New Jersey 08540

In the United Kingdom: Princeton University Press,
6 Oxford Street, Woodstock, Oxfordshire OX20 1TR

press.princeton.edu

Jacket illustration and design by Amanda Weiss

ISBN 978-0-691-17393-1

British Library Cataloging-in-Publication Data is available

This book has been composed in Baskerville 10 Pro

Printed on acid-free paper. ∞

Printed in the United States of America

3 5 7 9 10 8 6 4 2

If I am not for myself, who will be for me?

And if I am for myself only, what am I?

And if not now, when?

RABBI HILLEL

CONTENTS

MIDLIFE

INTRODUCTION

There is a tale of two great rabbis in the first century BCE. Shammai is strict, doctrinal, exclusive. His rival, Hillel, is just the opposite: humane, flexible, open. The story tells of a gentile who agrees to convert to Judaism on condition of being taught the Torah while standing on one foot. Dismissed with contempt by Shammai, the gentile comes to Hillel, who accepts him, saying, "That which is hateful unto you, do not do unto your neighbor. That is the whole Torah; all the rest is commentary. Now, go study."[1]

This book is written in the spirit of Hillel, whose words form its epigraph. Like the Talmud, philosophy can be forbidding and esoteric. This is nothing new: try reading Kant or Aristotle. Nor is it all bad. Hillel does not dismiss the more exacting forms of scholarship: he ends with the injunction to study. But he believes that the message of Judaism can be communicated simply and that it matters enough to be worth trying even at the risk of seeming naïve.

That is what I believe about philosophy. It could not survive without philosophers whose commitment to answering the most recalcitrant questions leads them into difficulty. But for all its disputes, uncertainties, and complications, academic philosophy has much to offer almost anyone in the midst of living, and wondering how to live, a human life.

My investment in this idea is personal, and not just because I teach philosophy for a living. I started thinking about midlife about six years ago, at the tender age of thirty-five. On the surface, life was going well. I had a stable family and career. I was a tenured professor in a good department housed in a congenial Midwestern city. I knew I was lucky to be doing what I loved. And yet there was something hollow in the prospect of doing more of it, in the projected sequence of accomplishments stretching through the future to retirement, decline, and death. When I paused to contemplate the life I had worked so hard to build, I felt a disconcerting mixture of nostalgia, regret, claustrophobia, emptiness, and fear. Was I having a midlife crisis?

You may protest that I was (and am?) too young for a midlife crisis. I appreciate the thought, though you should brace yourself for chapter 2. And in the end, I don't agree. What floored me were the existential questions of midlife, questions you are not too young to ask at thirty-five. You could ask them at twenty or at seventy, though I think they are especially salient when you reach my age. They are questions of loss and regret, success and failure, the lives you wanted and the life you have. They are questions of mortality and finitude, of emptiness in the pursuit of projects, whatever they are. Ultimately, they are questions about the temporal structure of human life and the activities that occupy it. This is a book not just for the middle-aged but for anyone coping with the irreversibility of time.

It is a work of applied philosophy: philosophical reflection trained on the challenges of midlife. And it takes the form of a self-help guide. The trials of middle age have been neglected by philosophers, but they are philosophically interesting, and they are amenable to therapy by the tools philosophers use. Until around the eighteenth century, there was no sharp line between moral philosophy and self-help.[2] Philosophers agreed that contemplation of the good life should make our own lives better. The divorce between these aims is a more recent innovation. Nowadays, few philosophers write self-help books. When they do, they mostly invoke the classics, often the Roman Stoics, Cicero, Seneca, and Epictetus, as though philosophy lost its relevance to life two thousand years ago. My approach is not historical. Though I mention past philosophers, ancient and modern, I do not treat them as sage-like repositories of wisdom but as interlocutors in working through the issues for myself— and, I hope, for you.

This book differs from standard self-help in part because it is more concerned with basic questions of how to feel about your life, in part because it is less concerned with outward change. For most of us, midlife is not too late to start something new, though it often feels that way. Don't be fooled by the foreshortening of time that accompanies middle age. You have more time than you think. That said, there are other books to consult for practical advice about career change at fifty or being single at forty-five. That is not the sort of advice I will give. But I will attempt to give advice, to communicate strategies for adapting to midlife inspired by philosophical ideas. Where the advice is familiar, I will explore the philosophy behind it. Where it is unfamiliar, I will argue that it is right.

In doing so, I assume no prior knowledge. I have tried to write a book that can be read while standing on one foot: technicalities are suppressed and I opt for brevity over completeness. The chapters that follow address what are, in effect, just some of the many midlife crises. There is the sense that life is too demanding, too consumed with needs, which is the focus of chapter 2. In resolving it, we will explore conceptions of reason, value, and the good life that owe their origin to Aristotle, and we will learn the importance of doing what you need not do. There is the sense of confinement in one's present life, however happy it may be, the acknowledgment of lost alternatives, which is the subject of chapter 3. We will learn how options are overrated and why there is something good about missing out. There is the sense of an imperfect, unchangeable past with which you must come to terms, in chapter 4. We will learn when and why you should be glad you made a mistake. There is the sense of time passed by, or running out, awareness of mortality, in chapter 5. We will engage with philosophical treatments for fear of death. And there is the sense of repetition and exhaustion in the succession of projects, day by day, and year by year, which is the subject of chapter 6. We will learn what it would mean to live in the present, how it could solve your midlife crisis, and why meditation helps.

Before we look for answers, we begin, in chapter 1, with a history of the question. We will investigate the stereotype of midlife as a time of crisis, unearthing its recent past. We will map its shifting present, its evolution from dizzying trauma to manageable malaise. And we will find a place for philosophy in its future. Contemporary philosophers have paid too little mind to aging, to the physical and temporal situations of childhood, midlife, and old age. It is time for that to change.

1

A BRIEF HISTORY OF THE MIDLIFE CRISIS

According to poet and librarian Philip Larkin, "Sexual intercourse began / In nineteen sixty-three / (which was rather late for me)."[1] We can date the origin of the midlife crisis with the same precision. In 1965, psychoanalyst Elliott Jaques published the essay that coined the phrase: "Death and the Mid-Life Crisis."[2] In dissecting the crisis, Jaques quotes a patient in his mid-thirties:

> "Up till now," he said, "life has seemed an endless upward slope, with nothing but the distant horizon in view. Now suddenly I seem to have reached the crest of the hill, and there stretching ahead is the downward slope with the end of the road in sight—far enough away it's true—but there is death observably present at the end."[3]

If you are reading this book, the odds are good that you relate to this moment. You know how you are supposed to feel, whether you feel that way or not. You have lived long enough to ask "Is that all there is?" Enough to have made some serious mistakes, to look back on triumphs and failures with pride and regret, to look sideways at lost alternatives, lives you did not choose and cannot live, and to look ahead to the end of life, not imminent but not so far off, its distance measured in units you now comprehend: another forty years, with luck.

You are not the first. We have contemporary models, like Lester Burnham in *American Beauty*, who quits his job, buys a fast car, and lusts after his teenage daughter's seductive friend.[4] But there are much earlier ones. A partial history would cite the protagonist of John Williams's luminous 1965 novel, *Stoner*, who at forty-two years old, with a failed marriage and stalled career, "could see nothing before him that he wished to enjoy and little behind him that he cared to remember."[5] No wonder he embarks on the prescribed affair. It would cite the absurd man of Albert Camus's 1942 *Myth of Sisyphus*, whose existential crisis is not timeless but comes "when a man notices or says that he is thirty."

> He admits that he stands at a certain point on a curve that he acknowledges having to travel to its end. He belongs to time, and by the horror that seizes him, he recognizes his worst enemy. Tomorrow, he was longing for tomorrow, whereas everything in him ought to reject it. That revolt of the flesh is the absurd.[6]

And it would cite *The History of Mr. Polly* by H. G. Wells, the darkly comic story of a bored shopkeeper whose abortive attempt at suicide makes him a local hero—he is credited with putting out the fire he started—and spurs him to begin life anew.[7] The book was published in 1910.

If representations of the midlife crisis precede its naming in 1965, how far can we trace the thing itself? It comes as a surprise to learn that Jaques's examples are largely drawn not from his clinical practice but from the lives of creative artists. He was struck by the frequency with which the age of thirty-seven, or thereabouts, brings either creative silence or transformation. By thirty-seven, Gioachino Rossini (1792–1868) had written his most successful operas, from *The Barber of Seville* to *William Tell*; though he lived another forty years, he barely composed again. At the same age, Johann Wolfgang Goethe (1749–1832) set off on a two-year journey through Italy. His greatest works were written afterwards, infused by the classics, as in the tragedy, *Faust*. Even Michelangelo (1475–1564) took a breather in midlife, painting virtually nothing from age forty to fifty-five, then the Medici monument and *The Last Judgment*.

It may strike you as reckless to speculate about the mental history of artists who died several centuries ago. We are not done yet. No stranger to reckless speculation, Philippe Ariès, the historian who posited the modern invention of childhood, traced the feeling of personal failure at midlife to the experience of "the rich, powerful, or learned man of the late Middle Ages" who had luxuries of aspiration denied to the inhabitants of traditional societies.[8] Think of Dante at thirty-five: "Midway on our life's journey, I found myself / In dark woods, the right road lost."[9]

Medievalist Mary Dove paints a very different picture in *The Perfect Age of Man's Life*, citing the Middle English narratives *Piers Plowman* and *Sir Gawain and the Green Knight*, which draw on Aristotle's theory of middle age as the prime of life, the body being most fully developed from thirty to thirty-five, the mind at forty-nine.[10] Others doubt that Ariès went far enough. In her 2002 book about the midlife crisis, *Regeneration*, psychotherapist Jane Polden takes as her paradigm the story of Odysseus in Homer's *Odyssey*.[11] Talk about a midlife crisis! Infidelity, drinking, the death of a beloved parent, and the need for some serious family counseling at the end. To be fair to Polden, she means it as a metaphor. The earliest text I have found cited as a genuine precedent for the midlife crisis is from Twelfth Dynasty Egypt, around 2000 BCE: a dialogue between a world-weary man and his soul—though as far as I can tell what he is weary of is the injustice that surrounds him, not the inadequacies of his own life.[12]

The moral of this prehistory is less the timelessness of the midlife crisis than the strength of its grip on our imaginations. It is all too easy to project our image of the crisis back into lives that are radically different from our own. The history I will tell in this chapter is not the imponderable history of midlife crises since the dawn of humankind, but the much more tractable history of the idea, from its inception in 1965 up to the present day.

Even as its popularity soars, the midlife crisis has been haunted by the charge that it is a mere projection, that there is really no such thing.

RISE AND FALL

Despite some notable precedents—including psychoanalyst Edmund Bergler's 1954 study of extramarital affairs, *The Revolt of the Middle-Aged Man*[13]—the midlife crisis was born in 1965. Its childhood was one of extraordinary promise and prodigious growth.

In 1966, Daniel Levinson, a psychology professor at Yale, embarked on a series of interviews with forty men aged from thirty-five to forty-five. He wanted to know if they shared his own midlife malaise. The result was a map of conjectured stages in adult male development, *The Seasons of a Man's Life*, published in 1978.[14] In the same year, UCLA psychiatrist Roger Gould published *Transformations: Growth and Change in Adult Life*.[15] He, too, was inspired by his own experience, a depression unexpectedly caused by the realization of a long-held dream: Gould and his wife had bought their own house in Los Angeles. Why was it making them so unhappy? Faced with personal trauma, Gould had the social scientist's response: he conducted a study, a self-assessment survey given to 524 people, male and female, aged sixteen to fifty. Like Levinson, Gould aimed to identify universal stages of development and growth, one of them the characteristic turmoil of midlife.

But it was 1976 that marked the coming of age of the midlife crisis, its cultural bar mitzvah. Two years earlier, journalist Gail Sheehy had talked to both Levinson and Gould for an article in *New York* magazine. She did not waste time. While they were pondering data, she wrote *Passages: Predictable Crises of Adult Life*, based in part on her own interviews with adults in their twenties, thirties, and forties.[16] The book was a huge hit. Since its publication, it has sold more than five million copies in twenty-eight languages, and in a survey of readers conducted by the Library of Congress in 1991, it was named one of the ten most influential books of the time.

Sheehy cited as her primary influence German psychoanalyst Erik Erikson, whose 1950 *Childhood and Society* was one of the first attempts to analyze human life, from birth to old age, as a series of distinct and consecutive stages.[17] Erikson had eight, each defined by its own conundrum: trust or mistrust during infancy, intimacy or isolation in early adult life, and in the second stage of adulthood, from thirty-five to sixty-four, generativity or stagnation. ("Generativity" was Erikson's term for emotional investment in future generations.) The influence of Levinson and Gould was more contested. Gould sued Sheehy in 1975, hoping to stop the publication of her book. He felt she had stolen his ideas, and eventually settled for $10,000 and 10 percent of royalties. Not a bad deal, in light of future sales. But the impact of Sheehy's book is not due simply to the fact that it came first. Sheehy had a knack for the memorable phrase—"the trying twenties," "Catch-30," "the Deadline Decade"— and a willingness to generalize that makes *Passages* read like a snapshot of American self-perception.

The snapshot is one in which the midlife crisis looms large. As we reach middle age, Sheehy argues, we have a sense of time running out. For women, the thirties and forties are a crossroads. Most had no college degree in 1974; their children were growing up and leaving home. They needed to imagine and begin a second life. For men, turning forty meant saying goodbye to impossible dreams, taming and rechanneling the ambition of youth. Whatever its fidelity, this narrative caught on. To the extent that things have changed, with greater equality in education, work, and family, the effect has not been to dislodge the stereotypes discovered or invented by Sheehy in 1976, but to make space for women to inhabit a stereotype once reserved for men: stalled career, fading youth, and listless marriage.

As to the prevalence of the crisis, Sheehy is non-committal, though she writes in general terms and clearly expects her readers to identify with her interview subjects. Others have been less reserved. In the preface to a neglected classic of midlife mythology, Barbara Fried's *The Middle-Age Crisis*, published in 1967, psychology professor Morris Stein wrote that the "crisis is ubiquitous":

> Each of us goes through it in his own way, experiences it with greater or lesser intensity, and emerges from it more or less reconciled to the years ahead.

It is a "natural" developmental crisis, and it is unavoidable.[18]

Scare quotes apart, the picture is one of social or biological fate. We are programmed for the midlife crisis, men and women alike, and the question is not whether but when. We had better be prepared.

By 1980, the idea of the midlife crisis was thriving, with a secure and prominent place in popular culture. It had become an idea that needs no explanation, the object of wry humor and knowing remarks. If you weren't having one yourself, you could read about the midlife crisis in countless novels, from *Something Happened* by Joseph Heller to Doris Lessing's *The Summer before the Dark*.[19] You could even play the board game. In *Mid-Life Crisis*, released in 1982, players choose whether to aim for stability, accumulate wealth, and manage stress, or declare a midlife crisis, racing headlong into bankruptcy, divorce, and nervous breakdown.

So much for perception. What about reality? The truth is, it was hard to know. We had the studies by Levinson, Gould, and Sheehy, but little systematic data. Easy to find anecdotal evidence of the midlife crisis if you ask around, but hardly scientific, and doubtless distorted, now, by the understandable tendency for people to explain themselves in socially salient terms. The idea of the midlife crisis is ready to hand, a tool for understanding and describing oneself to others, a tool especially attractive for its power to excuse what would otherwise be outrageous behavior. What do you expect? I'm having a midlife crisis!

The most significant challenge to the status quo began in 1989, with the establishment of the MacArthur Foundation's Research Network on Successful Midlife Development, directed by social psychologist Orville Gilbert Brim. The network brought together a team of thirteen researchers from a range of disciplines: psychology, sociology, anthropology, and medicine. Its major work: a vast study called "MIDUS"—Midlife in the United States—conducted primarily in 1995. MIDUS involved a survey administered to over 7,000 people aged twenty-five to seventy-four, with a forty-five-minute phone interview and a two-hour questionnaire. The survey instrument employed to analyze the data had over 1,100 items. This was big. And despite some predictable banality—according to one revelation, "physical health ratings become more negative over the midlife period"; who knew?—the MIDUS survey radically changed the social scientific orthodoxy. The result was that, around 2000, at the apt age of thirty-five, the idea of the midlife crisis was having a midlife crisis.

What did MIDUS say? In a 2004 collection, *How Healthy Are We?*, which Brim edited with two colleagues, psychology professor Carol Ryff and Ronald Kessler, professor of health care policy at Harvard Medical School, the results were carefully summarized, and the outlook is bright. "For the most part," we are told, "findings revealed a positive portrayal of aging: older adults reported higher levels of positive affect, combined with lower levels of negative affect relative to young and midlife adults."[20] It gets better: "age was negatively linked with major depression, with older adults showing less likelihood of this disorder."[21] The story is one of stability or improvement from youth to middle age and beyond. When the results were first made public, in 1999, the *Washington Post* ran a special section titled "Midlife without the Crisis." In the *New York Times* headline, "New Study Finds Middle Age Is the Prime of Life."

A follow-up study, led by Cornell sociologist Elaine Wethington and administered to 724 of the original participants, looked specifically at psychological turning points. Just 26 percent of those over forty reported having had a midlife crisis, with roughly equal proportions of women and men.[22] Hardly prevalent or pervasive. And even the figure of 26 percent was found misleading. Subsequent analysis revealed that those answering the survey used a highly elastic definition of the midlife crisis, applying the term to any period of difficulty in the relevant years. In other words, shit happens in midlife, with kids and parents, work and health. If you call it a midlife crisis, just because you can, then the midlife crisis afflicts about a quarter of all Americans. But it may have nothing to do with awareness of mortality, the finitude of life, regret about the past, lost opportunities, or failed ambitions—let alone with chronological age.

Other studies appeared to confirm the MIDUS verdict. In 2001, Margie Lachman, professor of psychology at Brandeis University, edited the *Handbook of Midlife Development*, a comprehensive doorstop of a book. According to one essay in the *Handbook*, "surveys routinely find individuals in midlife to have fewer psychological symptoms . . . higher levels of marital satisfaction, better life satisfaction and mastery . . . than younger individuals and, in general, to be in fairly good health."[23] According to another: "One of the most intriguing puzzles of life-span developmental psychology is the myth of a midlife crisis."[24] A new consensus was being formed, a new image of midlife as a time of competence and personal growth, not uncertainty or regression. By 2010, Susan Krauss Whitbourne, a trenchant critic of the 1970s stereotype, would include a whole section on "The Myth of the Midlife Crisis" in her book *The Search for Fulfillment*, based in part on a longitudinal study of 350 students at the University of Rochester in upstate New York.[25]

To some extent, the backlash against the midlife crisis was an overreaction to a caricature. The phrase can sound entirely negative: crisis as calamity. And there were claims for the prevalence of the crisis, as in the quote from Morris Stein above, that were unsustainable and empirically unfounded. The discoveries of the late 1990s spoke strongly against a narrative of widespread trauma. But the midlife crisis was never conceived as wholly bad, even by those most responsible for its description. From the very beginning, Elliott Jaques had linked the midlife crisis with transformation and creative rebirth. His essay was a corrective to George Miller Beard's *American Nervousness* (1881), which posits "neurasthenia" as the ailment of the educated classes and finds a rapid decline in artistic production from the age of thirty-nine.[26] Like Jaques, Sheehy saw in midlife the potential for positive change. Neither of them framed the crisis as a purely biological phenomenon, triggered by age alone, as opposed to the changing circumstances of midlife. And neither of them held that it was universal, or had to be universal in order to be real. A crisis that affects, say, 10 percent of adults from forty to sixty is a crisis worth thinking about.

There is no doubt, however, that the social scientific fortunes of the midlife crisis had declined. Scholars could now regard it as an urban legend, a popular fiction, not a psychological fact. If it was to flourish in its later years, it would have to reinvent itself, leave its partner in psychology, and change careers. That is exactly what happened. In need of a fresh start, the midlife crisis met the new economics of well-being.

LIFE BEGINS AT FORTY

There is an interesting history to be told about the shift in development economics from a virtually exclusive focus on gross national or domestic product to the wider range of measures now favored by national governments, the United Nations, and the World Bank. This is not the place to tell it. A highlight, from our perspective, is the work of Harvard economist and philosopher

Amartya Sen in the 1980s, which led to the adoption of the Human Development Index by the UN Development Program. Sen urged the measurement not of commodities but of capabilities, the achievement of human potential. The Human Development Index is a crude attempt to do this, combining GDP with life expectancy and educational attainment in a single number for each nation, first published in 1990. The next two decades saw an explosion of work in the economics of well-being, studying reports of momentary happiness and overall life-satisfaction in a variety of social and demographic contexts. Economics was no longer just about wealth.

One study in particular changed the fortunes, and perhaps the meaning, of the midlife crisis. In 2008, economists David Blanchflower at Dartmouth College and Andrew Oswald at the University of Warwick published an article, "Is Well-Being U-Shaped over the Life Cycle?"[27] They relied on surveys that asked adults of various ages, "All things considered, how satisfied are you with your life as a whole these days?" Adjusting for income, marital status, and employment, Blanchflower and Oswald found that the level of reported happiness by age had the shape of a gently curving U, starting high in young adulthood and ending higher in old age, with an average nadir at forty-six. The pattern showed up in seventy-two countries around the world. It was similar in men and women and regression analysis ruled out an explanation in terms of the stress of parenthood. The U-curve was pervasive, robust, and psychologically real. At forty-three years old, the midlife crisis had a new lease on life.

There was room for skepticism. In particular, a cross-sectional snapshot cannot refute a "cohort explanation" on which the U-curve is explained not by age and its attendant effects but by the similar life paths of people born at a given time. One might speculate, for instance, that the midlife crises of the 1960s were explained not by middle age itself but by the experience of reaching it in the eye of a counter-cultural hurricane in which one had no place. The crises of the present are inflected by growing inequality, recession, and the contraction of the job market. Social context matters. But Blanchflower and Oswald corrected for this. And the U-curve has been confirmed in longitudinal studies, which track the same individuals year by year.[28] The source of the U-curve is not differences in date of birth or the state of society but what happens when we age.

The most bizarre confirmation, of sorts, comes from a study of great apes that appeared in 2012.[29] Researchers asked zookeepers, volunteers, and caretakers to assess the mood, social satisfaction, and achievement of goals in two groups of chimpanzees and one group of orangutans, all of varying age. In a delightful turn, "Item four asked raters to indicate how happy they would be if they were the subject for a week." (Presumably, distressed to wake up in the body of an ape!) Despite the difficulty of answering such questions, consistency among evaluators suggests that the data are not subjective. Adjusting for sex and sample, the primatologists found that the level of happiness by age among great apes takes the shape of a gently curving U.

Perhaps the most striking thing about the article, published in the *Proceedings of the National Academy of Sciences*, is the title: "Evidence for a Midlife Crisis in Great Apes Consistent with the U-shape in Human Well-Being." Not surprisingly, the inflated rhetoric was echoed in media reports, from the *National Geographic* to the BBC, and in virtually every major newspaper: "Apes Have Midlife Crises, Too." On this new interpretation, the midlife crisis is a predictable dip in life-satisfaction as one reaches middle age, not the tumultuous angst of the original myth.

This is how we will picture the midlife crisis in the chapters to come. It is a phase of relative unhappiness that correlates with middle age. At the same time, the U-curve is not irrelevant to more extreme conditions. If average life-satisfaction is lowest at forty-six and there is a variation around the norm—a certain proportion of people being above average, a certain proportion below—we would expect emotional trauma to peak at roughly that age. That is what Blanchflower and Oswald saw. Looking at the incidence of depression and anxiety in a U.K. Labor Force Survey, they found that the likelihood topped out around forty-five, with a rate roughly four times that of teenagers and three times that of older adults. The chances of falling apart are significantly higher in midlife, even if the majority get by.

Attempts to explain the U-curve, though tentative, evoke the traditional stereotype. The most suggestive is due to German economist Hannes Schwandt. He studied longitudinal data tracking 23,000 people aged seventeen to eighty-five from 1991 to 2004. People were asked about their current level of overall life-satisfaction and about the level they expected to enjoy in five years' time. Schwandt learned that younger people tend to overestimate how satisfied they will be, while mid-lifers underestimate old age. Middle age is consequently worse than anticipated and at the same time hopes for the future fade. Hence the dismal vertex of the U-curve. Schwandt proposed a mathematical model in which experienced life-satisfaction is a function of how well life is going at the time, combined with optimism for the future and disappointment about the present. "As a whole," he writes, "these findings tell a story in which the age U-shape in job (and overall life) satisfaction is driven by unmet aspirations that are painfully felt in midlife, but beneficially abandoned and felt with less regret during old age."[30] The key to happiness, then, is managing one's expectations. (This seems like the right time to warn you that you are reading a very mediocre book.)

Schwandt's explanation resonates with Jaques and Sheehy, Levinson and Gould; it harks back to the pre-MIDUS paradigm. It has the feel of a satisfying middle ground. But not everyone is convinced. There is an ongoing controversy about the existence and significance of the fabled U-curve. Having declared the midlife crisis a myth, Susan Krauss Whitbourne ran her own survey of 500 adults that failed to replicate the midlife valley in overall satisfaction.[31] Whitbourne added two further tests, one asking respondents to evaluate how much they felt their current life had meaning, the other how much they were looking for that meaning. The search for meaning decreased in a straight line from people in their thirties to those in their forties, fifties, and sixties, and the presence of meaning steadily increased. When it comes to meaning in life, Whitbourne argues, aging is all good.

And so the midlife crisis reaches fifty, its health revived but its prospects unclear, just as I turn forty, a tenured professor with a wife and child, two books, and twenty-odd articles in print. I love the profession of philosophy but not with the fire I had ten years ago. The novelty of accomplishment is gone: first publication, first lecture, first day of class. I will finish the paper I am writing; it will eventually be published; and I will write another. I will teach these students; they will graduate and move on; I will teach more. The future is a tunnel of glass: the rest of life goes by, in its variety, elsewhere. My son will grow, my wife and I grow older. My body creaks and sags; back pain is a trusted companion, not a sometime visitor; I use a standing desk. My parents are getting on, their health increasingly precarious. I feel the finitude of life: the years are numbered; time is moving fast.

It could be worse. I could hate my job or have been fired from it, or both. My wife might have left me; I might want to leave her. I could be looking at a life that feels empty without children or one that is all too full of them. I might be living in conditions of poverty, famine, war. I recognize the luxury of the midlife crisis, with a degree of guilt and shame. Why can't I be more grateful for what I have? But this is my life. I am in the depths of the U-curve and I need help. Maybe you do, too.

This book tries to provide it, in a way. It is a self-help book in that it is an attempt to help myself, with the hope that what helps me will help you, too. It is an approach to the midlife crisis from the inside. And in the spirit of "write what you know," it is a philosophical approach. Is the midlife crisis ready for the second phase of creativity imagined by Elliott Jaques? Is it ready for "the emergence of a tragic and philosophical content" that yields, at last, to the serenity of old age?[32]

TRAGIC AND PHILOSOPHICAL

As our brief history shows, the enterprise of midlife studies has been an interdisciplinary affair. It has brought together doctors, social scientists, psychologists, journalists, and more. Notably absent, so far, have been philosophers. This despite the fact that they have been thinking hard about well-being and the good life since the dawn of Western philosophy in Athens, 2,500 years ago. Plato's *Republic* is a dialogue about the role of justice in the best human life. In the *Nicomachean Ethics*, named for his son, Nicomachus, Aristotle argued that a good life is one of virtuous activity in accordance with reason. His word for happiness or human flourishing, "*eudaimonia*," has been adopted by psychologists who distinguish self-realization or "eudaimonic well-being" from "hedonic well-being" or the experience of pleasure.[33] But what appears in this literature is a dismal caricature; Aristotle's arguments are not discussed.

I don't mean to complain. Philosophers have rarely addressed the midlife crisis, at least not by name, though they must often have experienced it. They have walked in the valley of the U-curve, but for the most part, they have not philosophized about it. (An honorable exception is Christopher Hamilton, whose compelling quasi-memoir, *Middle Age*, was one of the inspirations for this book.)

If the questions we associate with the midlife crisis are existential ones, questions about value and meaning in life, why have philosophers neglected them? I do not think it is an accident. Apart from disdain for the grimy facts of aging and bodily decay in much of Western philosophy, the problems of understanding middle age recommend themselves to other fields. Though there is work to do in the philosophy of social science, on the methodology and conceptual foundations of the kinds of inquiry pursued by MIDUS and others, philosophers have no special expertise in the empirical study of the midlife experience. And where the midlife crisis has a history, a social and demographic profile, varying by race, gender, and economic class, philosophers look for questions that feel timeless and universal. Plato and Aristotle ask "What is the best life for a human being?"

In the *Critique of Pure Reason*, Immanuel Kant, perhaps the greatest philosopher of the Enlightenment, insists that the "whole interest of . . . reason, whether speculative or practical," is encapsulated in three questions: "What can I know?", "What should I do?", and "What may I hope?"[34] Here the universality of the questions comes out, paradoxically, in their first-person character, as questions for anyone.

But despite appearances, these questions are not timeless. I do not mean that they have been understood in different ways at different historical moments, though that may well be true. I mean that they take particular temporal perspectives. When Kant asks "What should I do?" his orientation is prospective, forward-looking, and his mode pragmatic. When Aristotle asks "What is human flourishing?" he imagines looking back on a complete life from a standpoint outside it. The question of the best human life is a question asked about life as a whole. Thus Aristotle quotes the Athenian statesman, Solon, "Call no man happy until he is dead," and worries that this may not go far enough.[35] What happens after your death is not irrelevant to whether you lived the ideal life. "Poor guy," we might say of someone whose legacy is in tatters, "look what happened to the projects he began."

Neither the prospective question of what to do nor the external, retrospective question of the good human life captures the predicament of midlife. Neither is essentially situated within a life that has a meaningful past and a meaningful future, both of which you must confront. At midlife, retrospection is limited. You command a view of one substantial part but not the whole. And the question is not simply what to do, but what you have done and what you have not done, what to feel and how to think about yourself. There are distinctive problems that arise from the temporality of midlife, from our multiple orientations to the past and the future, from our relation to unrealized possibilities or counterfactuals, from the scale of life and of the projects that occupy it. These problems are obscured if we simply ask what to do and what would constitute an ideal life. They are the problems I will treat.

The treatment is a form of cognitive therapy. Despite the neglect of midlife in philosophy, there are philosophical insights that can illuminate middle age, that can free us from pathologies of value, show us when they are not inevitable, and reconcile us when they are. Philosophers have things to teach, as well as to learn, about the midlife crisis. My pursuit of these ideas is personal and introspective. Its method is not that of systematic social science but of attention to lived experience. What interest me are the questions symptomatic of the midlife crisis. How should we think about the lost opportunities, the regrets and failures, the finitude of life and the rush of activities that drive us through it?

Even if it is not widespread, the midlife crisis turns on temporal features of human life that are utterly pervasive: the progressive reduction of possibilities, completion or failure of projects, accumulation of biography. This mitigates somewhat the odor of self-indulgence in devoting so much thought to the plight of the affluent and entitled. According to Gail Sheehy, "It costs money to have a midlife crisis."[36] She is not entirely wrong. The U-curve shows up less in developing nations than it does in North America and Europe.[37] But while there may be moments in this book that have you reaching for the hashtag #firstworldproblems, its topics are quite general. We will trace their origins in our relation to the unknown, the counterfactual, the future, and the past.

This will entail some disappointments. Because I am interested in abstract questions of knowledge, value, and time, I will have less to say about fast cars and wild affairs. Not nothing, as you will see in chapter 6, but not so much. If that is a deal-breaker, I am sorry. (An appendix gives advice on how to seduce your next-door neighbor.) Nor will I address the social construction of the midlife crisis, its relationship to race, gender, and political circumstance. Philosophers may contribute to these questions, but they are not my primary concern. No doubt there are generational and geographic differences in the experience of midlife, in the depth and shape of the U-curve, but the challenges that will vex us are largely independent of that. They turn on the basic conditions of human life.

So, what to expect? Since the methods of philosophy are those of reflection and reasoning, there will be analyses and arguments. I cannot report on results established in the philosophy lab, asking that you take them on trust. There are no such results. Instead, like a student in grade school arithmetic, I will show my work. On occasion, we will follow a line of thought only to realize its limitations, and we will try to do better. If philosophy has authority, it is the authority of honest persuasion. As in psychotherapy, you should accept only what you can confirm yourself. The difference is that the therapist is a philosopher and the patient is a hypothetical victim of midlife. In constructing him or her, I will draw on my own experience and on case studies from Virginia Woolf to Simone de Beauvoir.

We turn first to a more unlikely subject: Victorian thinker and social activist John Stuart Mill. In exploring his nervous breakdown, a crisis at once epic and eccentric, I will introduce the methods of moral philosophy and its application to self-help. I will clarify the meaning of the midlife crisis by explaining what it is not, and I will diagnose and treat the first of its many forms. Mill's life is not a digression; his ghost will haunt us to the end.

2

IS THAT ALL
THERE IS?

The early life of John Stuart Mill was as remarkable as it was sad. He was born in 1806, the son of James Mill, a Scottish historian, political economist, and philosopher. James was a disciple of Jeremy Bentham, the first great moral utilitarian. In Bentham's infamous axiom, "it is the greatest happiness of the greatest number that is the measure of right and wrong."[1] Forget the past, ignore tradition: the institutions of society must answer to the interests of everyone they affect. What does not make us happier must change.

James Mill met Bentham in 1808 and was an immediate convert. His son, John Stuart, had not yet turned two. It was the beginning of an extraordinary experiment. On the principle that charity begins at home, James Mill designed the education of his son for the greatest happiness of the greatest number. He would be raised to make a difference in the world. The experiment was, in Isaiah Berlin's words, "an appalling success."[2] Success because John Stuart Mill went on to be the most influential British philosopher and public intellectual of the nineteenth century. Appalling for the loneliness and deprivation of his early years. Mill was sheltered from interaction with other children, and he was taught at an alarming pace: Greek at age three, reading Plato by seven; Latin at eight, Newton's *Principia* at age eleven; the teenage years spent on logic, political economy, psychology, and law; then Bentham and philosophy at fifteen. At the age of twenty, already an accomplished thinker, his father's son, John Stuart Mill had a nervous breakdown.

It may seem perverse to discuss Mill here, in a book about the midlife crisis, or to mine his experience for insights. He was quite young when he suffered the depression he recounts in his *Autobiography*. But in this, as in so many things, Mill was precocious. His crisis may be yours. It has the distinction of being exposed to sustained philosophical reflection. Mill tried to analyze his breakdown and recovery, drawing morals for moral philosophy: a precedent for my approach.

At the same time, I concede that some of what happened to Mill is not specific to midlife. Interpreting Mill's distress is the occasion for a crash course in philosophical ethics, setting the stage for the rest of the book. We will investigate the nature and pursuit of happiness. We will contrast the midlife crisis with a more radical collapse into nihilism. We will analyze the different kinds of value our activities can have. And we will find in Mill a crisis we could share. We may not have had childhoods like his. But perhaps we have groaned at the weight of what must be done, the hours consumed by necessity, at work and at home, and have asked ourselves, is that all there is? We will tackle that question, with help from Mill, below.

Despite its power, the narrative of Mill's depression has an inauspicious start. He chronicles his grief in terms both stark and unenlightening.

> I was in a dull state of nerves, such as everybody is occasionally liable to; unsusceptible to enjoyment or pleasurable excitement; one of those moods when what is pleasure at other times, becomes insipid or indifferent. . . . In this frame of mind it occurred to me to put the question directly to myself: "Suppose that all your objects in life were realized; that all the changes in institutions and opinions which you are looking forward to, could be completely effected at this very instant: would this be a great joy and happiness to you?" And an irrepressible self-consciousness distinctly answered, "No!"[3]

The mystery is *why*. Why should the achievement of one's deepest desires, one's most profound ambitions, be a matter of indifference? What has gone wrong?

You might say: quite a lot. Poor Mill, driven by his domineering father, the course of his career determined for him. How could he feel ownership of his life? A sense of autonomy or authenticity? No wonder Mill would later write *On Liberty*, his polemic for self-government and freedom of thought.

31

Then there is the feeling of isolation, the dearth of close relationships, the want of intimacy. In this respect, at least, Mill's story has a happy ending. In 1830, at the age of twenty-five, John Stuart Mill met Harriet Taylor, the love of his life. She was already married, but they became friends—Mill called it "the most valuable friendship of my life"[4]—and in 1851, after the death of her first husband, Mill proposed and Harriet accepted. In his *Autobiography*, Mill cites her as a virtual coauthor: "not only during the years of our married life, but during many of the years of confidential friendship which preceded, all my published writings were as much her work as mine"—including *On Liberty* and *The Subjection of Women*—though her "intellectual gifts did but minister to a moral character at once the noblest and the best balanced which I have ever met with in life."[5] Theirs is one of the great romances of both intellect and later life.

But for all its influence on his development, "in its detail, almost infinite,"[6] Mill does not credit his relationship with Harriet Taylor as the remedy for his breakdown, or point to loneliness as its cause. He does slyly hint at some parental difficulties, noting that "a small ray of light broke in upon my gloom [when] I was reading, accidentally, [Jean-François] Marmontel's *Memoirs*, and came to the passage which relates the death of his father, the distressed position of the family, and the sudden inspiration by which he, then a mere boy, felt and made them feel that he would be everything to them—would supply the place of all that they had lost."[7] Material for therapists, perhaps, but again, not part of Mill's self-diagnosis. Instead, he gives two reasons for his crisis, both of which repay attention, each of which has a philosophical past.

Mill reports two marked reversals in his thinking as his sentiments revived. The first is this:

> I never, indeed, wavered in the conviction that happiness is the test of all rules of conduct, and the end of life. But I now thought that this end was only to be attained by not making it the direct end. Those only are happy (I thought) who have their minds fixed on some object other than their own happiness; on the happiness of others, on the improvement of mankind, even on some art or pursuit, followed not as a means, but as itself an ideal end. Aiming thus at something else, they find happiness by the way.[8]

Mill's insight in this passage has a name: the paradox of egoism. And it has a history, dating back at least to sermons preached by Joseph Butler at the Rolls Chapel in London, which were published as a book in 1726.[9] An Anglican priest, Bishop Butler believed that egoism, or the exclusive pursuit of one's own happiness, would not only interfere with but logically preclude its own achievement. Like Mill post-reversal, Butler held that a crucial condition of happiness is caring about things other than oneself. This doesn't mean you have to be altruistic. What you care about might be baseball, or philosophy, or particular people, your friends and family, not humanity at large. When you care about something in this way, it is not just a means that you exploit for your own sake. Its flourishing makes you happy. And so the sources of happiness, though also of vulnerability, grow. That is Mill's idea.

I think it is a pretty good one. Call it the first rule for preventing a midlife crisis: you have to care about something other than yourself. If nothing matters to you but your own well-being, if you are utterly self-obsessed, not much will make you happy. In the basement of the U-curve, where satisfaction is hard to get, this fact is worth pondering. It is natural to respond by craving happiness more profoundly, setting it as your goal. The irony is that you need to do the opposite: you need to care about other things. This is not advice you can follow directly, since you cannot choose to love what leaves you cold. But it is not useless. You can choose to immerse yourself in things you might come to care about and so begin to change your life. Who knows, maybe reading about philosophy at midlife will inspire a new and abiding passion? I recommend it—though you may find other interests, too.

As well as pausing over the paradox of egoism, it is worth pausing to dismiss those cynics who deny that selfless desire is so much as possible. Commending themselves for a bitterly honest realism, these "psychological egoists" insist on reinterpreting apparently selfless behavior—the man who gives his life to protect imperiled artifacts, hiding their location,[10] the woman who donates a kidney to a total stranger[11]—as secret means to happiness. In doing so, they are forced to attribute motives and beliefs their subjects frankly disavow. For the most part, those who risk their lives for others don't believe they are doing it for their own good. Psychological egoism is a conspiracy theory of human motivation, and about as credible. A case in point is Mill himself, whose desire for social reform was never conceived as a plan for his own benefit. It persisted through the belief that its achievement would leave him cold. Even at the center of his despair, Mill did not stop wanting to transform the world or working toward that goal.

But this creates a puzzle. Whatever you make of the paradox of egoism, it is hard to see how it could apply to Mill. His problem was not undue devotion to himself. If anything, the opposite: Mill wanted nothing but the greatest happiness of the greatest number, counting his own life no more than any other. He did not need to learn the lesson of the paradox. And yet the crisis came. Mill's first diagnosis, though interesting in itself, is off the mark.

Perhaps ironically, it is tempting to cite in connection with Mill's breakdown not the paradox of egoism, but what might be called the paradox of altruism. I do not mean the alleged paradox of understanding how altruistic behavior is even possible, but the previously unnamed paradox implicit in Jackie Robinson's aphorism, "A life is not important except in the impact it has on other lives."[12] The young Mill might have agreed. But the idea is ultimately incoherent.

In order to see the incoherence, we need to borrow a distinction from moral philosophy, between final and instrumental value. Instrumental value is the value something has as a means to an end, like the value of making money or visiting the dentist. Worth doing, for sure, but only because the consequences of having money, or a root canal, are better than not. In contrast, what has final value is worth doing or having in itself, as an end, not just a means. It has non-instrumental value. Think of the value of happiness, for Bentham's utilitarian, something that is good even apart from its effects.

The suggestion in Robinson's remark is that the value of everything we do is instrumental: its value lies in its effects on others. But what is the value of those other lives and the activities that occupy them? If it, too, is instrumental, it depends on the value of its effects on others, and the value of those effects depends in turn on their effects on others, which depend in turn on their effects. . . . Value is perpetually deferred. As Aristotle insists at the very beginning of the *Nicomachean Ethics*, if the explanation of value is always instrumental, "the process would go on to infinity, so that . . . desire would be empty and vain."[13] It is only if human life matters in itself, apart from its effects, that there is any point in altruism. There is value in acting on behalf of others only if there is value in other activities, too. Hence the paradox: if altruism is the only thing that matters, nothing matters. Life is not worth living.

Am I being unfair to Robinson? Maybe so. He could have been making a point about the special kind of value that constitutes importance, not about what is good in human life. That would generate no paradox. But I am not the only one to worry about the perversion of altruism that fails to see the value of anything else. Think of the quip attributed to W. H. Auden: "The poet is capable of every conceit but that of the social worker: 'We are all here on earth to help others; what on earth the others are here for, I don't know.'"[14] (Auden got the joke from comedian John Foster Hall, "the Vicar of Mirth," who had been telling it since the 1920s.) It is not crazy to suspect that Mill's development had been warped by a self-denial that left him with little conception of the positive goals of altruistic endeavor. He was the social worker to Auden's poet.

But I don't think the paradox of altruism quite captures Mill's predicament. There is no reason to think Mill ever had doubts about the final value of meeting human needs. One aim of social reform is to reduce the scale of human suffering; the achievement of that aim has value in itself, apart from its effects. The projects of the social worker have more than instrumental worth.

If Mill evades the paradox of altruism, what about us? I hesitate to guess your character and I do not want

37

to cast aspersions, but in my own case I am sure that the midlife crisis does not turn on fanatical selflessness. Nor is it nihilistic. Even in its firmest grip, I know that there is reason to care for those I love, to do my job well if I can, to get things right, to be responsible, to help and not to harm. There is still value in the world.

No doubt reactions may be more extreme. In the crisis he recounts in "A Confession," Leo Tolstoy asks a version of the question that shook Mill, about the achievement of one's ambitions: "'Well, fine, so you will be more famous than Gogol, Pushkin, Shakespeare, Molière, more famous than all the writers in the world, and so what?'"[15] He had no answer. Tolstoy's downward spiral came later in life than Mill's—he was pushing fifty—and it went deeper. "My life came to a standstill," he writes, "I could breathe, eat, drink and sleep and I could not help breathing, eating, drinking and sleeping; but there was no life in me because I had no desires whose gratification I would have deemed it reasonable to fulfill."[16] It is possible to feel that way: that nothing is worth doing. But that is not how it was for Mill. It is not my experience. And I hope it is not yours.

The distinctive crises of midlife do not turn on a pervasive skepticism about reasons or values, on philosophical doubts so fundamental they owe nothing to the shape of human life. They do not invoke a comprehensive nihilism but more elusive conceptions of oneself and the world. That is why they are philosophically intriguing. It is a question for philosophy what distinguishes the emptiness of the midlife crisis from the unqualified emptiness in which one sees no reason to do anything, no reason to prefer one outcome to another. What is missing at midlife, if final value remains? The answers to this question call for distinctions in value, like the contrast of means and ends, though more subtle, more perplexing, and more poignant. We need a finer palette of ethical concepts with which to paint a philosophical portrait of midlife. The midlife crisis will be solved, in part, by conceptual pedantry.

So what was wrong with Mill? Not boundless egoism or the conclusion that nothing matters. Still, there is something in the paradox of altruism. There is something in the idea that Mill's obsessive attention to social reform left a void in his conception of happiness, a void that could afflict anyone, including you. That is what Mill himself came to believe. In order to see why, we must turn a critical eye to the second great reversal in his thinking, to a diagnosis of Mill's breakdown that sounds a quiet, unmarked echo of Aristotle.

MAKE YOURSELF IMMORTAL

What Mill calls the "other important change" in his opinions was that "for the first time, [he] gave its proper place, among the prime necessities of human well-being, to the internal culture of the individual."[17] By this he meant the expression and refinement of human feelings in the appreciation of art.

There is some doubt about the aesthetic merits of Mill's own writing. Fellow Victorian, Thomas Carlyle, to whom Mill credited the paradox of egoism, advised a friend in 1872, "You have lost nothing by missing the autobiography of Mill. I have never read a more uninteresting book . . . [the] Autobiography of a steam-engine."[18] But it is hard to be unmoved by Mill's account of reading, two years after his mental crisis, the poetry of William Wordsworth.

> What made Wordsworth's poems a medicine for my state of mind, was that they expressed, not mere outward beauty, but states of feeling, and of thought coloured by feeling, under the excitement of beauty. They seemed to be the very culture of the feelings, which I was in quest of. In them I seemed to draw from a source of inward joy, of sympathetic and imaginative pleasure, which could be shared in by all human beings; which had no connexion with struggle or imperfection, but would be made richer by every improvement in the physical or social condition of mankind. From them I seemed to learn what would be the perennial sources of happiness, when all the greater evils of life shall have been removed. And I felt myself at once better and happier as I came under their influence.[19]

Mill was especially taken with Wordsworth's "Ode: Intimations of Immortality from Recollections of Early

Childhood." He went so far as to compare Wordsworth's experience to his own: "he also had felt that the first freshness of youthful enjoyment of life was not lasting; but . . . he had sought for compensation, and found it, in the way in which he was now teaching me to find it. The result was that I gradually, but completely, emerged from my habitual depression, and was never again subject to it."[20]

I do not begrudge Mill his recovery: whatever works for you. But the comparison is strained. When Wordsworth exalts "Delight and liberty, the simple creed / Of Childhood," he is not thinking of a childhood like Mill's! The crucial fact is not that their lives were similar, but that the poetry of nature was, for Mill, a source of distinctive value, the culture of the feelings that is Wordsworth's closing theme:

Thanks to the human heart by which we live,
Thanks to its tenderness, its joys, and fears,
To me the meanest flower that blows can give
Thoughts that do often lie too deep for tears.[21]

People complain about Wordsworth's writing, too. Mill concedes that "even in our own age, [there are] greater poets."[22] (What is up with that redundant verb in the final line, apparently dictated by the meter?) For Mill, Wordsworth is "the poet of unpoetical natures."[23] At the same time, he insists, "poetry of deeper and loftier feeling could not have done for me at that time what his did."[24] Through Wordsworth, Mill was "made to feel that there was real, permanent happiness in tranquil contemplation."[25] To Mill's unpoetical nature, this came as a revelation.

What exactly did Mill learn about the value of art, and what does it have to do with us, mired as we may be in the malaise of middle age? To answer these questions, we will need to look a little further back, to the most articulate champion of tranquil contemplation, the ancient Greek philosopher, Aristotle. Equipped with Aristotelian tools, we will be able to fashion a second rule of midlife crisis prevention.

Aristotle, who lived from 384 to 322 BCE, was a student in Plato's Academy in Athens. Plato nicknamed him, playfully, "*noûs*," which means mind or intellect. The life of the mind plays a curious role in Aristotle's thinking. A disorienting fact about the *Nicomachean Ethics*—the set of lecture notes I have mentioned twice before—is that they spend nine "books" or chapters on the practical virtues, such as courage, temperance, and justice, only to end, in Book X, by demeaning the practical life in favor of pure intellect. Generations of readers have been baffled by the bait-and-switch, and scores of interpreters have tried to explain it away.

The interesting thing is how closely Aristotle's reasons for disaffection with the life of practical virtue match the reasons given by Mill for his turn to the culture of the feelings.

Now the activity of the practical virtues is exhibited in political or military affairs, but the actions concerned with these seem to be unleisurely. War-like actions are completely so (for no one chooses to be at war, or provokes war, for the sake of being at war; anyone would seem absolutely murderous if he were to make enemies of his friends in order to bring about battle and slaughter); but the action of the statesman is also unleisurely, and aims—beyond the political action itself—at despotic power and honours, or at all events happiness, for him and his fellow citizens—a happiness different from political action, and evidently sought as being different.[26]

Like Mill, Aristotle is concerned that the activities of practical virtue—fighting wars, engaging in politics, working for social reform—are sustained "by struggle and privation."[27] Their worth depends on the existence of problems, difficulties, needs, which these activities aim to solve. In an ideal world, there would be no use for them. That is why it would be insane to make enemies of friends in order to create the opportunity for courage in battle. Equally lunatic, Mill might add, to foster human suffering in order to make work for reformers like him.

Aristotle is quite clear that the achievements of the statesman have final value. They "are desirable both in themselves and for the sake of [another] thing": "a happiness different from political action, and evidently sought as being different."[28] He did not spend nine books of a treatise about the good life on mere instruments, the equivalent of dental care and getting rich quick. But for

Aristotle, the value of political action is ameliorative, the value of a double negative: responding to injustice, suffering, war, it extinguishes something bad. Better still would be a world in which there is no need, nothing broken to repair, no injury to heal. That is the limitation and the defect of practical virtue, for Aristotle, why it is absent from the ideal life. Like social work and political reform, in Mill, its purpose turns on "struggle or imperfection," conditions we would rather do without.[29]

Is there room for a more positive vision of politics, on which it does more than mitigate harm? Might our statesman fund the arts, the pursuit of basic science, or philosophy itself? Perhaps. But Aristotle will complain: whatever help we get from the state, it would be better not to need. Nor does amending our theory of politics tell us which activities the statesman should support.

That is where contemplation comes in. To contemplate, for Aristotle, is not to solve theoretical puzzles, let alone to apply our theories in practice, but to reflect on answers we already have. This activity "alone would seem to be loved for its own sake," he writes, "for nothing arises from it apart from the contemplating, while from practical activities we gain more or less apart from the action."[30] In Aristotle's terms, the contemplative life is "final without qualification": "desirable in itself and never for the sake of something else."[31] This can sound bizarre, as though we should prize contemplation for being useless. What is so great about that? But what matters to Aristotle is not that contemplation serves no purpose but that its value is wholly positive. It does not respond to trouble or imperfection, to suffering and strife, but is gloriously redundant. It is not something we need to do in order to prevent injustice or harm, but something we would want to do even in an ideal world. Unlike political action, contemplation is leisurely, "[and] happiness is thought to depend on leisure; for we are busy that we may have leisure, and make war that we may live in peace."[32]

Though he does not refer to Aristotle, Mill must have read the *Ethics*, most likely in Greek at the age of ten. The question that vexed Mill—how would you feel if your reforms were instantly realized?—evokes the Aristotelian contrast between ameliorative value and the positive worth of contemplation. If injustice could be eradicated, if human suffering was dissolved, what would be left for us to do? Before his nervous breakdown, Mill had no idea. Though his activities had final value, they were not final without qualification. They were addressed to regrettable human needs.

In the wake of the crisis, this changed. In poetry, Mill found "a source of inward joy [that] had no connexion with struggle or imperfection."[33] Its pleasures were not those of hardship overcome but would be "perennial sources of happiness, when all the greater evils of life shall have been removed."[34] The problem with Mill's earlier life was that it gave no hint of what is worth doing except to reduce the scale of human suffering. If the best we can hope for is not to suffer, to live a life that is not positively bad, why bother to live life at all? If value is always ameliorative, there may be things we should care about in themselves, as ends not just as means, but life as a whole is not worth living. Better, or just as good, not to be born.

Like me, you may not be fanatically selfless. You may not be an Athenian statesman, either. But modern life can have the defect that disturbed both Aristotle and John Stuart Mill: it can be crowded with demands, with bills to pay, mouths to feed, problems to solve, preoccupied by "struggle and privation."[35] Think of the days on which you have nothing to look forward to but sleep: a respite from childcare, putting out fires at work, fighting to keep your relationships alive. Don't get me wrong, these things all matter. Their value may be final; but it is essentially ameliorative. Caught on the treadmill of what has to be done, day by day, you may not have time for what you want but do not need. In the words of Mill's near-contemporary, German philosopher, Arthur Schopenhauer,

> Work, worry, toil and trouble are indeed the lot of almost all men their whole life long. And yet if every desire were satisfied as soon as it arose how would men occupy their lives, how would they pass the time?[36]

This is what you ask yourself when you lose all conception of what is worth doing except to prevent things from going wrong or make them right. It is a variation on Mill's question. "Work, worry, toil and trouble": unavoidable, sure, but is that all there is?

Crises of this kind come by degree; they rise and fall. Your life may be more or less consumed by amelioration, more or less awash with needs. There may be pockets of leisure in which to breathe. Or the crisis may emerge as demands on your time recede—perhaps the kids are growing up—and you realize the void, your days no longer filled by what must be done, though there is not much else to do.

This is one version of the midlife crisis. Like Mill's nervous breakdown, it is not nihilistic. It turns on the grinding necessity of work, not the absence of value from the world. What needs to be done is well worth doing. But something is left out. To describe what is missing, we need to distinguish, among activities that have final value, between ones that are not just ameliorative and ones that are.

Despite their love of impenetrable jargon, philosophers have not evolved a terminology for this contrast, which is why I have been reduced to wordy circumlocution. ("Not just ameliorative" is a triple negative: not merely such as to prevent or extinguish something bad.) It is not my fault. The distinction we have drawn from Aristotle and Mill has been neglected in moral philos ophy. We need a term for what is not-just-ameliorative. Since it makes life positively good, not merely better than it could be, and so explains why life is worth living at all, I call such value "existential." Hence the second rule: in your job, your relationships, your spare time, you must make room for activities with existential value.

This may sound rather grand, especially since our main example of existential value is the value of tranquil contemplation. Are you condemned to read Wordsworth or to reflect, with Aristotle, on the rational order of the world? Not quite. For existential values are more varied and more down-to-earth. Although they both use "contemplation," Mill and Aristotle have very different things in mind. Aristotelian contemplation is an exercise of understanding made possible by the completion of scientific inquiry: it is reflection on the structure of the cosmos with God as final cause. Mill is thinking of poetic appreciation and more generally of art. (Aristotle cites "artistic contemplation" only once in the ethical works, as something you can do with friends.)[37] What these activities have in common is their non-ameliorative worth. Once we see this, we can open the door to other activities whose value is existential. What matters is that they do not turn on unfortunate features of human life. Examples range from philosophy and high art to telling funny stories, listening to pop music, swimming or sailing, playing games with family or friends. These activities may respond to difficulties in life; they may distract you from suffering or merely pass the time. But each can be "a source of inward joy" unconnected with struggle and imperfection; a perennial ground of happiness when "the greater evils of life shall have been removed."[38]

Have we swung from grandiosity to bathos? From contemplating God and nature to taking up a fun new hobby? Yes and no.

No, because it is not just hobbies that have existential value. You can find it at work, too, or in relationships with others. I have the incredible good fortune of a job in which I am paid to think and write: activities whose value, if any, is existential. (I suppose there is a chance that in writing this book, I will reduce the scale of human suffering. But that is doubtful, and I am sure you could not say it of my other books.) Other jobs contribute to making things, material or otherwise. Aristotle would deny that their value is existential: they solve problems of need. In an ideal world, furniture and food would grow on trees. But this is of a piece with his blindness to the value of art. We do not have to agree with him. We can insist that carpentry and cooking could be part of an ideal life, that if they turn on human needs, they are not needs we would be better off without. Work can have existential value. The same is true of friendship, which confuses Aristotle because he is convinced that contemplation is the only existential good. (The best friends are ones who can help us contemplate, though if we could do without them, presumably we should.) We need not think that way ourselves. Even in an ideal world, we might decide to spend time with friends.

On the other hand, it is true that much valuable work is ameliorative. We need doctors, teachers, and social workers. And it is true that hobbies can have existential value. Midlife is the time to take up golf, the most existential of all activities, or salsa dancing, or playing piano. Instead of feeling let down by the mundanity of our adjustment to middle age, we should see things the other way around. Our idle pastimes are more profound than we may have thought. When Aristotle maligns the life of practical virtue, he illustrates its flaws by imagining the gods, who have no need to ameliorate anything: "We assume the gods to be above all other beings blessed and happy; but what sort of actions must we assign to them? Acts of justice? Will not the gods seem absurd if they make contracts and return deposits, and so on? . . . And what would their temperate acts be? Is not such praise tasteless since they have no bad appetites?"[39] (The joke is that the Olympian gods are constantly bickering, indulging, and sleeping with mortals; for Aristotle, these are no gods.) Activities of existential value are fit for immortality: they could belong to an ideal life. When you play Monopoly with friends, or read a book for pleasure, you have a share in the life of the gods.

Let me end by saying what this does not mean. It does not mean that existential value matters more than anything else, that it should always come first. Aristotle's view is perilously close to that.

> But we must not follow those who advise us, being men, to think of human things, and, being mortal, of mortal things, but must, so far as we can, make ourselves immortal, and strain every nerve to live in

accordance with the best thing in us; for even if it be small in bulk, much more does it in power and worth surpass everything.[40]

I don't agree with Aristotle. When the demands of life are pressing, too urgent to be ignored, it would be a mistake to devote all day to contemplation, reading Wordsworth, or playing golf. Being mortal, think of mortal things.

Yet if you lose touch with existential value, if you find no place in your life for the activities of the gods—ones that make life worth living to begin with—you risk a mid-life crisis not unlike John Stuart Mill's. If you have the opportunity, you should make yourself immortal, some of the time.

SHADES OF THE PRISON-HOUSE

What have we learned from Mill? That a crisis lies in wait for those whose lives lack existential value, who aspire at most to mitigate harm, as though the absence of suffering is as good as it gets. That is an awfully pessimistic view. It took a childhood like Mill's to conceal the pleasures of poetry, to obscure the value of doing anything except to benefit those in need.

There are more commonplace crises, too. Less bleak than Mill's, they turn on a relative absence of existential value, the sense that there is not enough of it, not that there is none at all. The pressures of work and family are so consuming they obscure the possibility of doing anything else. If this is your life, you need to make room for activities with existential worth. They may be less important than doing your job or making the sure the kids are fed, but they have value of a different, irreplaceable kind.

I said before that there are many midlife crises. We have been addressing one of them, a crisis of necessity, inspired by John Stuart Mill. There is some irony here. For the poet who showed Mill how to solve his early crisis had a crisis of his own. He did not share Mill's optimism. Mill cites the "Immortality Ode" as a model for his own recovery, perhaps recalling lines like these:

> To me alone there came a thought of grief:
> A timely utterance gave that thought relief,
>   And I again am strong.
> The cataracts blow their trumpets from the steep.[41]

But the trumpets sound early in a poem whose next stanza ends: "Whither is fled the visionary gleam? / Where is it now, the glory and the dream?" Some recovery! The air of nostalgia and loss is constantly recycled as Wordsworth's poem returns, again and again, to the freedom of childhood constrained by the "prison-house" of society.

What about the last four lines? A celebration of feelings inspired by nature, as Mill supposed? Much more ambivalent. It is tears, not smiles, that our thoughts lie too deep for. And that extra verb it is so easy to mock?

"Thoughts that do often lie too deep for tears" enacts the depth of thoughts that can be captured only clumsily in words, and the contrivance and oppression of social norms, as feelings must conform to metrical rules. Even poetry is marred by the blinders of civilization, graffiti on the prison wall.

Wordsworth did not recover from his midlife crisis. After finishing the first full version of *The Prelude* at thirty-five, he was creatively spent, writing little of note in his last forty years. Nothing could "bring back the hour / Of splendour in the grass." You need not share with Wordsworth the belief in an immortal soul, incarnate in birth, "trailing clouds of glory . . . / From God, who is our home," to feel nostalgia for the spacious world of youth, the open future, unconfined. There is no return. But we can ask what it is we miss about the time before our lives acquire the definite shape they have at thirty-five, or at fifty, the age at which, for Orwell, "everyone has the face he deserves."[42] What is the value of having options and how should we come to terms with ones that we have lost? Can we find "Strength in what remains behind; / . . . In years that bring the philosophic mind"? In the next chapter, with help from both novelists and philosophers, that is what we will try to do.

3

MISSING OUT

When I tell friends I am working on the midlife crisis, I wait for the jokes to subside, then ask for reading suggestions. What I get are mostly novels, mostly by men. Some I have mentioned already; some we will get to in time. Others range from the comic (Richard Russo, *Straight Man*) to the bleakly comic (Saul Bellow, *Herzog*) to the bleak (Richard Yates, *Revolutionary Road*).[1] By and large, they share the stereotype of middle age as a period of lost opportunity, frustrated longing, and oppressive social constraint. Midlife is missing out.

Some friends reply with fact, not fiction, finding the now conventional narrative in their own biography. A note from a successful colleague:

> For what it's worth, I came closest to having a mid-life crisis when I turned 40 in the middle of 1994. . . .
> Everything was going incredibly well in my life. But with three very young children and a huge mort-gage, I had the vivid sense that there was no way that I was ever going to change direction and . . . oh, I don't know . . . write a novel, or make a movie, or

become a folk singer, or whatever it was I had always fantasized I could do if I wanted to. I was locked in to doing what I was doing forever, by the sheer force of the need to generate an income of a certain level, and that depressed me no end. Of course, this was incredibly self-indulgent, and [my wife] was having none of it. But I now find it strangely comforting to think that it might be a literary genre!

There is comfort in numbers, in recognition, familiarity a preface to comprehension. When it comes to missing out, is there a better consolation? We have to face facts. In my case, these. . . .

In the beginning, I wanted to be a poet. I wrote my first real poem at the age of seven: rhyming couplets that evoked the desolation of the playground, T. S. Eliot meets Ogden Nash. I won't pretend it was any good. I began to take things more seriously in a workshop taught by Carol Ann Duffy, now poet laureate, at the time much less well-known. She made us write sonnets from the point of view of characters assigned by drawing scraps of paper from a hat; the first four lines had to describe what they could see through a window. I picked "fashion model." I was a twelve-year-old boy, and someone else got "astronaut." Daunted and embarrassed, I tried, probably for the first time, to imagine the world through someone else's eyes. Duffy liked the poem, I liked writing it, and I liked the fact that it was like nothing I had written before. But I did not become a poet.

For a while, I thought about medicine. My father is a doctor and he wanted one of his sons to continue the family business. He drew inspiration from a 1980s sitcom, *Don't Wait Up*, about father-son dermatologists. Dermatology was promising, he thought, because few patients die. I was more interested in saving lives, though I faint at the sight of blood. When push came to shove, I followed my muse, and applied to read philosophy. So here we are.

I don't regret my decision. I don't believe I would have lived a better life in poetry or medicine; most likely, worse. I have been very fortunate. I am lucky to have a tenured position in philosophy at a time of financial duress in academia; even luckier to be sheltered by the wealth and stability of MIT. I am lucky to have wonderful colleagues and students. If you are hoping for catastrophe, you will have to wait. Chapter 4 is about how to feel when things go wrong; this is the chapter in which we complain when things go right. For in spite of everything, when I run the experiment, draw "doctor" or "poet" from the hat of personal history, trace a branch in the tree of possibilities now cut off, I feel a sense of loss that is not unlike regret. There are the poems I will never write, the lives I will not save. I see no path from where I am to those alternatives, no future in which I go to medical school or become a good enough poet. (No doubt, dear reader, you are wishing I were more of one.) Even if I did, it would not be the life that I imagined at seventeen. I look back with envy at my younger self, options open, choices not yet made. He could be anything. But I am condemned: course set, path fixed, doors closed.

This is not a flattering portrait. It is indecent to whine that one cannot have it all. But there may be something in it. Perhaps you conjure, too, the spirits of lives unlived, the things you could have done but never did and never will. You don't have to think you made a mistake to feel that you missed out, or to experience nostalgia for a time when you did not know what shape your life would take. If I could write about you, I would. An advantage of using myself, apart from practicality, is that my story is so dull. The idea of vocation that shaped my planning lends the stylized simplicity of a thought experiment to an actual life. The average forty-year-old has had thirteen jobs and is looking to move at any time.[2] Her tree has more branches, a fractal intricacy inherited by the lives she has not lived. Mine is conveniently pruned. Three branches—poet, physician, philosopher—one living, two dead, a singular, reductive instance of a fact in any human life: the fact of missing out. Can philosophy help us come to terms with this? Can it teach us to accept what we cannot have? And to work through, or understand, the lure of nostalgia that surrounds the loss of youth? In this chapter, I argue, within limits, that it can.

THE LIFE OF A MOLLUSK

As so often, the first contribution of philosophy is to make a distinction and give it a name. Not all decisions evoke the sense of loss that is our theme; we need to distinguish ones that do from ones that don't.

Suppose you are offered a financial prize and you have to choose how much: you can have one fifty-dollar bill or you can have two. Other things being equal, I assume you would take the hundred dollars, and you would not give your choice a second thought. You would feel no inner conflict in making the decision, and it would leave no residue of disappointment or regret. It would be absurd to mourn the lost opportunity for less. The value of your options is, in one sense of a much-abused term, commensurable.

Commensurable values are measured on a single scale; the greater subsumes and compensates for what is less. There is no basis for unsatisfied desire in turning down one fifty-dollar bill, since the desire that explains why you would want that bill, the desire for money, is better met by taking two.

Decisions of this kind are comparatively rare. Suppose, instead, that you must choose between hearing a lecture on a subject that interests you—interstellar travel, say, or the history of the Russian doll—and attending the birthday party of someone you recently met and would like to get to know. You are torn, though you decide that, on balance, the party matters more. And so you go. Unlike the choice of a hundred dollars, this decision entails uncompensated loss. The value of knowledge and the value of friendship are incommensurable, and while you may be justified in choosing the latter here,

the greater value does not subsume the lesser. The desire
that explains why you want to hear the lecture will not
be met at the birthday party. It lingers, unsatisfied, in
your heart.

This may seem overly dramatic. You will not be tor-
tured by the memory of the missed lecture. But incommensurability can be more intense. In William Styron's
1979 novel, *Sophie's Choice*, a mother is made to decide,
on her arrival at Auschwitz, which of her two children
will live and which will die; if she refuses, they will both
be killed.[3] She elects to sacrifice her daughter. Her subsequent life is devastated by guilt, though it is hard to see
what better choice she had. The value of one child's life is
incommensurable with the other. In a well-known essay,
Jean-Paul Sartre describes a student who came to ask
him for advice. Should he risk his life in the resistance or
take care of his mother, who will otherwise be desperate
and alone?[4] There is no way to avoid incurable loss.

The clearest cases of commensurability involve
means, like wealth, that we apply to further ends. In
principle, though, there could be commensurability in
final value. Jeremy Bentham, whom we met in chapter 2, understood happiness, "the measure of right and
wrong," in terms of a "felicific calculus" that balanced
units of pleasure against mitigating units of pain.[5] He
treated pleasure as a homogeneous sensation, an eval-
uative buzz, more of which is better than less. In John
Stuart Mill's memorable misquotation, "quantity of
pleasure being equal, push-pin is as good as poetry."[6]

(Push-pin was a British children's game played in the nineteenth century.) Choosing between two pleasant experiences, for Bentham, is like choosing between two piles of money. You should opt for more without a second thought. The pleasure you receive subsumes and compensates for the pleasure you decline. You miss out on nothing, since what you get is more of the same. Yet unlike the value of money, the value of pleasure is final. According to Bentham, enjoyment is the primary end of human life.

Does terminology help? When I think again about the things I haven't done, the verse unwritten, lives unsaved, how much comfort do I get from saying that the values of poetry, medicine, philosophy are incommensurable? And what about you? Do you feel better, now, about the path your life has taken, the fact of missing out? Probably not.

But wait. There is another way to view our situation. Why do we face the problem of unsatisfied desire, even when things go well? Why is midlife missing out? That we cannot have everything we want, and what we have does not subsume or compensate for what we don't, is a consequence of incommensurability. It follows from the diversity of values in human life, from the fact that there are so many different things worth wanting, worth caring about, worth striving and fighting for, too many ever to exhaust. Only blindness to much that is of value or a pathological narrowness of taste could save you from missing out. And no one should want that.

Try to imagine what life would have to be for you to avoid irreparable loss. When you face incompatible options, their values must be commensurable or one of them must mean nothing to you. You could not love poetry, medicine, philosophy all at once. Most of what is good in human life must be occluded or expunged. Your affective experience will be monochromatic: no inner conflict, but none of the variety of emotional life from which it stems.

You might hope to follow Bentham, grasping for a hedonistic scheme, a felicific calculus in which the only good is pleasure minus pain. But Bentham's theory does not convince, not just because there is more to life than how it feels, but because even pleasures are often incommensurable. Forced to choose between watching the sunset and hearing a symphony, you may decide to listen; but it makes sense to be conflicted. The desire to see the colors of the setting sun will not be satisfied by the sound of music. What we want are particular pleasures, not a homogenous hedonic buzz.

To achieve commensurability, you must forgo variety or differentiation in kinds of pleasure. You must care only for the quantity, not the quality or object of your enjoyment. Your desires must be radically simplified, by the annihilation of most of what is good, or by your indifference to it. "You would thus not live a human life," as Plato writes in the *Philebus*, "but the life of a mollusk or of one of those creatures in shells that live in the sea."[7]

To wish for a life without loss is to wish for a profound impoverishment in the world or in your capacity to engage with it, a drastic limiting of horizons. There is something to be said for this. In a reflexive instance of incommensurability, it makes sense to be conflicted about incommensurability itself, which is in one way bad. But it would be perverse to prefer, on balance, the diminishment required to repair the harm.

What we learn from this is not a rule for avoiding the midlife crisis, but advice for coping with it. There is consolation in the fact that missing out is an inexorable side effect of the richness of human life. It reflects something wonderful: that there is so much to love and that it is so various that one history could not encompass it all. Even immortality would not suffice: your biography must have a determinate shape that differs from other eternities you could have lived. You still miss out.

So tell yourself this: although I may regret regret, desire that no desire go unfulfilled, I cannot in the end prefer to have desires that could be fully met. The sense of loss is real; but it is something to concede, not wish away. Embrace your losses as fair payment for the surplus of being alive.

UNDERGROUND MEN

There are limits to this result. For one thing, it does not help us to avoid the problem of missing out, only to accept it. As cognitive therapy, it aims to change how we think and thus how we feel about a circumstance, not to change the circumstance itself. Nor does it address the sort of regret that is not inevitable: regret about mistakes, misfortunes, failures, in which life turns out worse than it could have done.

We will confront adversity in chapter 4. Before that, a more glaring omission: nothing I have said so far explains the temporal dimension of missing out, its connection with nostalgia. Why look back with longing at the time before one's course was set? Why envy youth? Not because you had everything: not getting what you want is the constant refrain of childhood. And if you had not yet missed out on more profound desires, it was already certain that you would.

The mystery of nostalgia is one of several explored in a recent novel by Joshua Ferris, *To Rise Again at a Decent Hour*. It is the story of a man adrift, committed to nothing but the Boston Red Sox, an atheist nostalgic for the absolute, for religious language and community, a novel about the plight of the individual in liberal society, about the dislocations of freedom and modernity.[8] It is also, as Janet Maslin wrote in the *New York Times*, "a highwater mark in the literature of dentistry."[9]

Being British, I am well attuned to the literal and metaphorical import of the cavity. Unlike wrinkles and middle age spread, the rotting of teeth is the visible disintegration of the body, the overt mark of cumulative, irreversible decay. Teeth do not repair themselves, like bones, but steadily erode, as though part of one's skull were exposed to view, already dead or dying. Is it a coincidence that Dostoevsky's Underground Man, that icon of existential angst, once had a toothache for a month?[10] Some years ago, at a convention of philosophers in a large hotel, I asked one of the staff what she thought we were. She answered "dentists"—an implausible guess in light of all the beards, and not intended as a compliment. Perhaps she could sense that we, too, gaze into the abyss.

The fact of physical decline, which teeth make palpable, is one we can try to ignore, like Ferris's narrator, "whistling past the grave of every open mouth."[11] Or we can hope to reverse it, like Martin Amis, who spent part of his advance for *The Information*, a novel about a midlife crisis, on massive dental reconstruction.[12] But it is only a matter of time. "Looking in the mirror now, on the morning of his fortieth birthday," writes Amis of his protagonist, "Richard felt that *no one* deserved the face he had."[13] If not at forty, then at fifty, or at sixty, the body shows its age.

I wish I could tell you that philosophy will halt this process, will suspend biological entropy. It will not. As well as an appendix on seduction, this book needs an appendix with three quick tips for smoother skin, firm abs, and a brighter smile. Maybe the next edition? If the image of your youthful body, now long gone, inspires nostalgia, if you envy the face you see in photographs from 1996, my best advice is to be wistful in advance. As Nora Ephron writes: "Anything you think is wrong with your body at the age of thirty-five you will be nostalgic for at the age of forty-five."[14] The method of proleptic nostalgia: imagine how you will feel about the face in the mirror, the body you inhabit today, when you look back from ten or twenty years. It could and will be worse.

The problem is not just losing your looks. What we mourn for in lost youth is only in part cosmetic. Aging brings, too, a depletion of energy, stamina, vitality. Physical capacities fade. Aging is a corporeal symbol of the progressive diminution of prospects. Youth, in contrast, stands for undiminished powers and a future as replete with possibility as it will ever be. When I think about missing out, when I envy myself at seventeen, this is what I picture. It is the object of my nostalgia.

There is a puzzle here that Ferris brings to light. Observe his aimless dentist, Paul O'Rourke, persuading himself not to have a child:

> Now *there* was something that could be everything, I thought: kids. From the moment they're born, until the time is right for them to gather around you for your final word, and every milestone in between. But for them to be everything, they would also have to *be* everything: no more restaurants, Broadway plays, movies, museums, art galleries, or any of the other countless activities the city made possible. Not that that was an insurmountable problem for me, given how little I'd indulged in

them in the past. But they lived in me as options, and options are important.[15]

What is the value of having options you do not exercise, paths you do not walk? For Paul, "[every] night was a night of limitless possibility expired, of a life forfeited, of a foreclosed opportunity to expand, explore, risk, hope, and live."[16] He declines the opportunity in order to preserve for himself more opportunities he will not take. It makes no sense!

How different is Paul's perversity from my nostalgia? It seems natural to want one's future open, one's opportunities intact. But on reflection, it is hard to explain why. If all goes well, the options you take are no worse than those you reject. (We are setting aside mistakes, misfortunes, failures, just for now.) So what have you lost? Why should I look back with envy at the time before I chose philosophy, when I could have been a doctor or a poet, if I do not believe that I went wrong? What do I gain by the expansion of possibilities I won't pursue?

The best way to kill a joke is to explain it, so with apologies, here is an argument—inspired by moral philosopher Gerald Dworkin[17]—that explains what is funny about Paul. (It is mildly technical, which also kills the humor. But what we lose in comedy we gain in understanding.) Imagine there are three outcomes, A, B, and C, that you rank in that order. If you were to be assigned an outcome, you would prefer A to B and B to C. Now suppose that having options is important, as Paul believes: the existence of alternatives has final value, in addition to the value of the alternatives themselves. It follows that having B and C as options is better than just getting B, with no alternative. That sounds fine. What is odd is that, if A is only slightly better than B, and there is value in having options, it could make sense to prefer a choice between B and C to just getting A, even though you prefer A to either B or C, considered alone. The value of the choice is the value of B, which you will choose, plus the value of having options; if this value is greater than the difference between A and B, considered alone, having the choice of B and C is better than just getting A. But that is absurd! Who would prefer a choice between alternatives each of which is worse than A to getting A itself?

This is not a rhetorical question. Having reveled in his toothache, the Underground Man adopts the preference I have called absurd, dismissing "wiseacres" like me: "What has made them conceive that man must want a rationally advantageous choice? What man wants is simply *independent* choice, whatever that independence may cost and wherever it may lead. And choice, of course, the devil only knows what choice."[18] When you share a preference with a man who enjoys a toothache, you know that you have gone astray. Options do not have the value Paul imagines.

All of which points to the puzzle promised above, a puzzle about nostalgia when it is directed, like mine, at the wider possibilities of youth. If I do not regret the way my life has gone, what is the appeal of having alternatives, as I once did? Why wish for options that I would not take? Am I simply confused?

Don't answer yet. Instead, consider what the argument from Ferris and Dworkin shows. It places a limit on the value of having options. It would be foolish to prefer a choice between B and C to just getting A if you would prefer A to either B or C, considered alone. But it could still be rational to want options: to prefer a choice between B and C in which one chooses B to having no alternative.

There are good reasons to wish for choice or for its absence. The meaning of an outcome may depend on whether there were alternatives, for good or ill, and its value may consequently change. Part of what is awful about Sophie's dilemma is that, whichever child she picks, she could have saved, even though one of them was bound to die. In this case, it is worse to be made to choose than to have no alternative.

A happier illustration is the life of Reginald Perrin, the subject of a novel by David Nobbs that inspired a memorable television series.[19] For those not immersed in British sitcoms of the late 1970s: Reggie Perrin flees his repetitive, drone-like job at Sunshine Desserts, fakes his own death, abandoning his clothes and suitcase on a beach, only to return after copious misadventures disguised as "Martin Wellbourne," who marries Reggie's "widow" Elizabeth and is hired to replace him at work. What is the point of this comically elaborate iteration? What does Reggie mean to prove?

What, indeed? That he was not just a product of Freudian slips and traumatic experiences and bad education and capitalist pointlessness? That he was more than just the product of every second of every minute of every day of his forty-six years? That he was capable of behaving in a way that was not utterly predictable? That his past was not his future's gaoler? That he would not die at a certain minute of a certain day that had already been determined? That he was free?[20]

At the risk of killing another joke, what Reggie flees is not his life, which though absurd is about as good as any other, but the sense that he has no alternative. His genius is to undo the ropes of his mundane existence only to retie the knot, transformed by the expression of will. Reggie's marriage to Elizabeth and his job at Sunshine Desserts mean something different at the end than at the beginning, however similar they look. They are a world he has chosen, albeit with irony, not a prison he can't escape.

Reggie Perrin is a joyful riposte to Paul O'Rourke and the Underground Man. He values having options enough to defy convention, not enough to sacrifice the better outcome for a choice among worse. He slips through the gap in the argument above as if it were made for him. He is an existential hero.

He is also an example for me to mind in my nostalgia. It does makes sense to wish for options, to resent the confinement of one's position, even when things go well. There is no way now to be a poet or a doctor of the sort I once conceived. If I choose to go on with philosophy, it is not with those alternatives but with others more constrained. In that respect, the meaning of my choice is different from the meaning of my choice at seventeen. Something has been lost. Midlife is missing out not just on other lives but on the meaning for one's present life of having them as options. Like the colleague quoted at the start, I want to do my job because I want to do my job, not because I need to pay the bills.

At the same time, there is a risk of being fooled, of mistaking a deficit that turns on the loss of possibilities for a defect in the outcome one is living. It is not wrong to lament the limitations of midlife, but it is a confusion to think that they justify radical change, trading in A for a choice between B and C, which makes things worse. The fact is that, absent the ingenuity of Reggie Perrin, your decisions in middle age cannot mean what they did twenty years ago; and even Reggie can't reverse the passage of time.

So, more advice from philosophy, if not another rule. Tell yourself this: while there are reasons to change one's life—frustrating jobs, failed marriages, poor health—the appeal of change itself can be deceptive. Because there is value in having options, you will miss having them: an argument for nostalgia. But the value is easy to overrate. It is silly to think that having options could make up for reaching outcomes you would not prefer, considered alone. Think twice before you wreck your home. Is it the space inside you hate, or the fact that it has walls?

CONSOLATIONS

We have one last thread to unravel, which brings together past and present, nostalgic yearning and frustrated wish. Our story began with the inevitable fact of missing out, by middle age, on meaningful desires. "You can't have everything," quips stand-up Steven Wright, "Where would you put it?"[21]

Nor is the fact of missing out news. It was true of me at seventeen that I would have to decide which to pursue—poetry, medicine, or philosophy—and I knew it. Despite my dad's insistence, I would not be happy to read philosophy, or write poems, on the side. But though I was aware that something had to give, I did not feel the loss as I do now. A further cause for envy: my younger self was sheltered, somehow, from the ache of unsatisfied desire. At midlife, we are exposed.

What explains this shift in perspective? Why does the affective cost of missing out increase, when it was fated from the start? An obvious change is that my losses were once future; now they are present or past. What were then lives I would not live are ones I am not living and never did. But while time's arrow has its part to play in the midlife crisis, as we will see in chapter 5, the nostalgia of missing out is not, in the end, a temporal phenomenon.

We can bring this out by further reducing my already simple life. Imagine I had to choose a career, irrevocably, at eighteen. It is a difficult decision, for as soon as I make it, I am in a position to feel the loss that troubles me now. I experience deprivation in prospect, reflecting on the poems I will not write, lives I will not save. That my losses are yet to come does not protect me from dismay.

Even in my actual, unsimplified life, the reversible decision to do philosophy brought something like regret, for the futures I was setting aside. What I envy about myself at seventeen is not that I had all this ahead of me, but the time before I had to choose, before I knew what my losses would be. In philosophers' terms, the shift in perspective is not temporal, but "epistemic": it has to do with knowledge. Emotionally, there is a fundamental difference between knowing that I will miss out on something good and knowing *what*, knowing that I won't achieve all of my ambitions and knowing *which*. It is when I know that I won't be a poet or a doctor that I feel the pain of missing out, and not before.

Or rather, it is when I am actually deciding, when I deliberate in earnest, that I experience conflict. And it is not just me. There is empirical evidence that we struggle with choices that involve uncompensated loss. In a 2001 survey of consumers deciding which car to buy, with different pros and cons, "researchers concluded that *being forced to confront trade-offs in making decisions makes people unhappy and indecisive.*"[22] This finding is robust: it shows up in study after study.[23] Choosing between incommensurable values elicits, conditionally and prospectively, the perception of unsatisfied desire. No wonder it is aversive. And no wonder we are reluctant to make decisions, anticipating discontent no matter how we choose.

What connects nostalgia with missing out is not that there was a time when we could have everything, but that there was a time before we had to commit ourselves and thus confront our losses. In practice, the commitment comes gradually, not in some immutable contract signed at age eighteen; options attenuate over time. It is easy not to notice until it is too late. And so I find myself at forty, imagining my carefree days at seventeen, when I did not know what I would be missing.

Still, whatever its allure, which I have attempted to explain, there is something unreal in this depiction of youth. It overlooks the major disadvantage of not knowing what you will not do: not knowing what you will. One way to expose the perversity of the nostalgic impulse is to imagine other ways of meeting it. If what I want is not to know what I am missing and therefore not to feel its loss, why not wish for retrograde amnesia? What I had at seventeen I could regain by forgetting what I have done, perhaps remembering that I am a poet, physician, or philosopher, but not remembering which. Strange as it may seem, there is an attraction to this prospect, an emotional reprieve. There is a reason to envy my amnesiac self that echoes nostalgia for the opportunities of youth. What I envy is not his future, but his relative freedom from regret. On the other hand . . . I doubt that you would choose amnesia if you could, and nor would I. To state the obvious: losing one's memory would be traumatic, in part because it would involve a calamitous loss of identity. Who am I? What am I doing with my life?

We should not forget that the same is true, in part, of being seventeen. Not knowing what you will do with your life may be liberating, but it induces vertigo. Writer Meghan Daum evokes this ambivalence in a recent essay:

Now that I am almost never the youngest person in any room I realize that what I miss most about those times is the very thing that drove me so mad back when I was living in them. What I miss is the feeling that nothing has started yet, that the future towers over the past, that the present is merely a planning phase for the gleaming architecture that will make up the skyline of the rest of my life. But what I forget is the loneliness of all that. If everything is ahead then nothing is behind. You have no ballast. You have no tailwinds either. You hardly ever know what to do, because you've hardly done anything. I guess this is why wisdom is supposed to be the consolation prize of aging. It's supposed to give us better things to do than stand around and watch in disbelief as the past casts long shadows over the future.[24]

Afflicted with nostalgia, even as things go well, it is wise to recall the desolation of the playground: the uncertainty, confusion, hope, and fear.

I submit that nostalgia for lost alternatives is distorted by hindsight. Looking back from a place of relative stability, I project into my youth a degree of assurance that comes from having a more or less secure identity. At the same time, I assume an open future, an ignorance of what is to come that shields me from unsatisfied desire. But the prospect is an illusion. You can't have it both ways, knowing who you are but not who you are not.

The upshot is a final bit of cognitive therapy. If, like me and Wordsworth, you are nostalgic for the indeterminacy of childhood, when almost anything was possible, tell yourself that what you long for is akin to retrograde amnesia. It would require a similar dissolution of the structure that gives meaning to your life. Its appeal is delusory. Beside this we can put two prior maxims: that you cannot be saved from missing out except by an appalling diminution of the world or your response to it; and that the value of having options is too limited to justify throwing your life away.

Thus concludes a first attempt to use the tools of philosophy in dealing with one's past: the paths not taken, lives unlived. To some extent, nostalgia for youth and regret at missing out turn on mistakes about value or a failure to think through the implications of one's desires. They are apt for philosophical treatment of the sort this chapter supplies. I can't say how much comfort you will derive from the arguments I have made; I can only hope. But I can say with sincerity that these ideas have been helpful to me as I negotiate the transition to middle age.

I anticipate a protest. Philosophers, who like nothing more than to refute each other, will be quick to remind you that I have made things easy for myself. After all, I stipulated that the life in question, yours or mine, is going well. We were to ignore, for the present, regret that one's life has turned out badly, marred by mistakes, misfortunes, failures. The real challenge is not accepting that I will never be a poet or physician when I am sure that philosophy was not the wrong decision. It is accepting that I can never take back the things I should not have said or done, that I cannot change the past events that have impaired my life, that I do not get a second chance. Philosophy may offer consolation for the idle complaints of the most fortunate. What can it do for the rest of us? Have philosophers evolved or identified technologies for managing regret in its more bitter and encompassing forms? In chapter 4, we will learn that the answer is yes.

4

RETROSPECTION

Mistakes, misfortunes, failures: choices you should not have made, hardships you should not have faced, plans that did not turn out as they should. No one makes it to midlife without acquiring some of each. The question now is what to do with them. How to feel about the ways in which life is not what you hoped it would be? Philosophy cannot change the past. But it can help us to accept it. In this chapter, I will try to explain how.

Before we start, I need to address a preemptive skepticism. Hearing our question—how to feel about mistakes, misfortunes, failures?—some will feel that the answer is depressingly clear. Short of self-deception or wishful thinking, what attitude can we take to such events except to wish, devoutly and unequivocally, that they had never taken place? What can we do but pointlessly prefer that history be rewritten? If only I had told the truth, the test had come back negative, I had waited one more year, things would be different, and better, than they are. It is futile to obsess about the past and time may dull the edge of anger or shame. But there is no merit in being dishonest. Who does not admire the brusque integrity of Frank Bascombe, the sportswriter of Richard Ford's 1986 novel?

> For now let me say only this: if sportswriting teaches you anything, and there is much truth to it as well as plenty of lies, it is that for your life to be worth anything you must sooner or later face the possibility of terrible, searing regret. Though you must also manage to avoid it or your life will be ruined.[1]

The advice is: don't screw up. Once you do, it is too late.

But it is not too late, not necessarily. In Faulkner's often mangled aphorism, "The past is never dead. It's not even past."[2] There is a difference between mistakes, misfortunes, failures, on the one hand, and regrets, on the other. We can pull apart what you should have done, or wanted, or welcomed at the time from what you should prefer in retrospect. This is clear when outcomes are unexpected. Philosopher Jay Wallace gives a neat example.[3] Suppose I have promised to drive you to the airport, but on the day of the flight, I can't be bothered to get up. You miss the plane, only to discover later that it crashed over the ocean, killing everyone on board. In breaking my promise, I did something I should not have done; but looking back, I don't wish I had done otherwise, and neither do you!

The distinction here is not especially subtle, but it is often missed. In *Regret: The Persistence of the Possible*, psychologist Janet Landman cites a Gallup poll conducted in 1949, which asked a national sample of adults to identify "the biggest mistake of your life so far."[4] Sixtynine percent were willing to admit to one. The winner, by some margin, was not getting more education, mentioned by 22 percent of respondents. Ten percent said they had made mistakes in marriage; eight percent said they had chosen the wrong job. In 1953, Gallup conducted another poll: "Generally speaking, if you could live your life over again, would you live it in much the same way as you have, or would you live it differently?"[5] Less than 40 percent of people said they would live life differently if they could do it again. Landman cannot explain this momentous decline. Did Truman cut the rate of regret dramatically in just four years? A miracle! But the questions asked by the polls are simply different. The first is about mistakes, things you should not have done. The second is about regrets, things you would take back now, if only you could. In taking them back, you erase not only the mistakes, but everything in your subsequent life that flowed from them. A more disturbing prospect: no wonder the numbers dropped. Regretting a mistake is not just admitting that you screwed up, but wishing that you hadn't, that you could subtract your mistake from the record of history, along with its effects.

So there is a glimmer of hope. Even when we make mistakes, endure hardships, see our efforts fail, we can aim for the space between honesty and regret, between acknowledging the past for what it is and wanting to rewind it to the point at which things went wrong. In principle, at least, we do not need a time machine to mute the regrets that occupy midlife. What we need is a rational way to shift our perspective on past events in light of their relation to the present. In what follows, we will explore the prospects for doing this, starting with more straightforward moves and conceding their limitations, before attempting to vindicate tactics at once more powerful and more puzzling. By the end, I hope you will have found some strategies you can use.

A TEMPORARY CONDITION

To warm up, consider a fictional version of me, who lacks the nerve for philosophy, with its dismal job market, and ends up an accountant instead. Suppose—with apologies to accountants who may be reading—that this is clearly a mistake, given what I know. I am acting against the evidence, which suggests that I will find accounting a tedious occupation, remunerative but mind-numbing. Yet imagine, in a miraculous obverse of the unexpected plane crash, that this prediction is entirely wrong. Years later, I find myself nodding to the words of David Foster Wallace, in a note that accompanied the manuscript of his final, unfinished novel:

> It turns out that bliss—a second-by-second joy and gratitude at the gift of being alive, conscious—lies on the other side of crushing, crushing boredom.

80

Pay close attention to the most tedious thing you can find (tax returns, televised golf) and, in waves, a boredom like you've never known will wash over you and just about kill you. Ride these out, and it's like stepping from black and white into color. Like water after days in the desert. Constant bliss in every atom.[6]

This is my (fictional) experience as an accountant: conducting audits, checking files, submitting tax returns, endlessly, repetitively, an alchemy of unspeakable boredom transformed into limitless joy.

A simple way not to regret your mistakes is to have things turn out better than you hoped. There was no way I could have known, in advance, the epiphany to come. But now that I have had it, I am glad of the mistakes that made it possible. If you think through your life, you will likely find events that fit this pattern, from the trivial to the grand. Error is part of the human condition: things turn out better or worse than you had reason to expect, redeeming a bad decision or ruining a good one. (The same is true of events that are not decisions, things that happen to you that were not things you did.)

On the other hand, having things turn out for the best is not much of a plan. It is not up to you, not something you control. It is not a matter of perspective but of luck. So, while simple in itself, the loophole of the unexpected consequence is of little use to the occupant of middle age, struggling to accept the past. It doesn't help Natalie—Nat, for short—who quits a promising but precarious career as a musician to become a corporate lawyer, whose job holds few surprises, and who is inclined to second-guess her youthful choice. It doesn't help the man who knows his marriage was ill-advised and has watched it fail, like the narrator of Hanif Kureishi's *Intimacy*: "That first time she put her hand on my arm—I wish I had turned away. Why didn't I? The waste; the waste of time and feeling."[7]

This is the more interesting, more difficult case, the one you may need help with. How to assuage regret about things you should not have done, or that you hoped would not occur, when they have turned out as you had reason to believe they would? What if there is no pleasant surprise? Does anything else subtract from the ledger of discontent?

Turns out it does. In recent philosophy, recognition of this fact can be traced to a thought experiment made famous—at least among philosophers—by a philosopher about as famous as any of us get to be. Derek Parfit was born in China to missionary doctors; he went to school at Eton, studied Modern History at Oxford, then turned to philosophy at twenty-three. In 1967, Parfit won a coveted "Prize Fellowship" at All Souls College, where he remained for fifty years. With the eccentric habits, flashing eyes, and wild white curls of the mad scientist, Parfit cut a romantic figure, compelling enough to be the subject of a somewhat baffled profile in the *New Yorker*.[8] We will meet him again in chapter 5, thinking about death. In 1976, he was thinking about new life.[9]

In Parfit's arresting hypothetical, you have a medical condition that will affect any child you conceive in the next three months. The child will be born with a serious, incurable disorder that affects his quality of life: chronic joint pain, say, or recurrent migraines. Since there is no urgent reason to conceive right now, Parfit concludes that you should wait. The immediate puzzle is why. After all, if you conceive and give birth to a child, he cannot complain that he would have been better off if you had waited. He would not exist at all! You would have had some other child, months or years later, if you had become a parent then. What matters for us, however, is not this puzzle, which has many solutions, but your attitude toward the past. Here is your son, growing, thriving, struggling. His life is good on the whole, though marred by predictable suffering. Back when you could, you should have chosen to wait. But now? Can you regret your decision? Should you wish to rewrite the past, erase your son's existence, and start over? There is pressure to say no.

You should have waited, but you are glad you didn't. What explains, what justifies, this shift in attitude? There is no great mystery. It is the existence of your child that makes the difference. You love your son, who is happy to be alive; and if you had waited, he would never have been born. It is the value of human life, crying out for affirmation, that silences the murmur of regret. You made a bad decision, but even though it has turned out as you feared—no sudden twists in the aftermath—you have reason to embrace the past. That reason has a name: it is the name of your son.

From here, it is a short step to the wistful lawyer and Kureishi's broken marriage. Nat has no David Foster Wallace revelation. Practicing law is as boring as expected in the usual, boring way. How can she not regret her decision to leave music, not to fight for a career as a pianist, when she loved playing so much? We have an answer, now, in theory. If Nat has a child, she can tell herself this: "There is no denying that the work is dull: there are jobs that I'd prefer. But if I hadn't gone to law school, I would not have met my husband, Al, and if I hadn't met him, my daughter, Sam, would not have been conceived. If I had stuck with piano, she would not exist. Loving her as I do, I cannot wish for a second chance. I don't deny that there is loss involved in living this way— though a wise man told me loss is inevitable—but I don't regret it overall, and I don't think I should." Kureishi's protagonist, Jay, can say the same thing: if he had turned away, the son he loves would never have been born.

We are making progress. One way to shield mistakes, misfortunes, failures from regret is to have things turn out better than expected. But even when they don't, regret is not compulsory. The words I have put in the mouth of our bored attorney do not pronounce some esoteric intellectual trick, but a perfectly intelligible way to reconcile with the past. Parents, try it for yourselves, if you have not already. Troubled by regret in middle age, ask yourself this: of the lapses and adversities that lie in the history of my child's conception, ones without which it would not have taken place, which do I accept as the price of her existence? These are aspects of the past that you cannot regret, even though you should have deplored them at the time.

How effective is this cure? It has definite limitations. Unlike Jay Wallace, author of the unexpected plane crash, I do not believe that affirmation of those we love, and of the histories that led to them, should be unconditional.[10] Wallace is led by this commitment to make extraordinary claims: if I love my son and he would not exist if the Holocaust had not occurred—my wife's maternal grandmother fled Germany in 1938—I must affirm Hitler's rise to power, even as I recoil from it, in a state of insoluble conflict.[11] On a more moderate view, which I prefer, the power of attachment can be defeated. If past events were sufficiently awful, attachment is at most a partial counterweight to regret, enough to complicate but not to overturn it.

Another limitation: the tactic we've discovered only works for past events on which the conception of a child depends. How much of an impediment is that? The good news: as chaos theorists tell us—citing the so-called butterfly effect—even quite minor alterations in the past would produce quite different futures.[12] A lot of what you did and what occurred to you before your son or daughter was conceived meets the condition it needs to meet:

they owe their life to it. The bad news: once the child is born, you are on your own. If subsequent disasters are to be redeemed, it will have to be by other means.

All of which points to the greatest drawback of appealing to new life as a remedy for regret. In ordinary circumstances, it is a ploy available only to biological parents and then only for a number of years. To take the most direct exception: it gives us nothing at all to say when the object of potential regret is the decision *not* to have kids. Does philosophy side with a sentimental vision of children as the antidote to disappointment, a singular ground of meaning that repairs the wreckage of the past? Or is comfort to be found elsewhere, consolation for the childless—and for parents, too—that does not turn on luck or on the value of procreation? That question is far from easy to address.

INSTEAD OF A CHILD

We are not the first to ask it. In the diaries she kept throughout her life, Virginia Woolf returns, again and again, to parenthood: her decision against it and the divergent life of her sister, Vanessa Bell. From an entry dated January 2, 1923:

> We came back from Rodmell yesterday, & I am in one of my moods, as the nurses used to call it, today. And what is it & why? A desire for children, I suppose; for Nessa's life; for the sense of flowers

breaking all around me involuntarily. . . . Years &
years ago, after the Lytton affair, I said to myself,
walking up the hill at Beireuth, never pretend that
the things you haven't got are not worth having;
good advice I think. At least it often comes back to
me. Never pretend that children, for instance, can
be replaced by other things.[13]

In Woolf's case: novels. Six years later, *Orlando* is praised
as a "masterpiece" in the *Manchester Guardian*, and Woolf
revisits her loss.

Orlando is recognized for the masterpiece that it
is. The Times does not mention Nessa's pictures.
Yet, she said last night, I have spent a long time
over one of them. Then I think to myself, So I have
something, instead of children, & fall comparing
our lives. I note my own withdrawal from those
desires; my absorption in what I call, inaccurately,
ideas: this vision.[14]

An actual life is not a thought experiment; a sister is
not a counterfactual self. But Woolf's problem is ours.
Can attachment to activities, like writing, or artifacts,
like *Orlando*, play the role that children play as medicines
for regret? Can Woolf echo the wistful lawyer? What
would she say?—"Perhaps I should have tried to have
a child; it is difficult to know. But I cannot regret that I
did not. If I had become a mother, I would have had less

time to write, more anxieties, more distractions. Some of my books, at least, would not exist. Loving them as I do, I cannot wish to revise the past."

In between attachment to one's child and attachment to mere things is attachment to human beings you did not create, ones whose existence does not depend on you. A further question: how far can relationships make up for what would otherwise be regret? Woolf touches on this theme in *To the Lighthouse*:

> And what was he groaning about, she asked, half laughing, half complaining, for she guessed what he was thinking—he would have written better books if he had not married.
>
> He was not complaining, he said. She knew that he did not complain. She knew that he had nothing whatever to complain of. And he seized her hand and raised it to his lips and kissed it with an intensity that brought the tears to her eyes, and quickly he dropped it.[15]

It is not clear that this case fits our model, since Mr. Ramsay may not have gone astray: he may believe that the benefits of marriage outweigh the costs. But we can imagine otherwise. Suppose Nat is childless, and that she is pragmatic enough to believe that if she hadn't met her husband, she would have been just fine. She would have married someone else or been happily single. On the other hand, she loves Al, and she would not have met him if she had not studied law. Can she cite their relationship as a reason to embrace her misguided choice?

In 1979, philosopher Robert Adams published a brilliant essay, "Existence, Self-Interest, and the Problem of Evil," that answered yes, yes, and yes: attachment to activities, artifacts, relationships, can justify retrospective affirmation of events we should have not have welcomed at the time. He compares such devotion not to parenthood but to the way in which we affirm our own existence.

> What we are attached to in ourselves, in a reasonable self-concern, is not just our bare metaphysical identity, but also projects, friendships, and at least some of the most important features of our personal history and character. If our lives are good, we have the same sort of reason to be glad we have had them rather than lives that would have been even better but too thoroughly different, as we have to be glad that we exist and not better and happier people instead of us.[16]

I don't know about you, but this passage feels to me both wise and weirdly perplexing. If Nat is happy enough, the suggestion runs, it makes sense for her to prefer her actual life—with her husband, Al, and friends, her hobbies and interests, virtues and vices—to lives that would have been better for her, and better overall. Perhaps that is right, but how? How can it be rational to prefer what you think is worse? Adams may be voicing some deep truth about the human condition, but if we leave it here, if we have no more to say, this truth remains obscure. In the final section of this chapter, I will explain what I take the truth to be. Before that, a closer look at why it eludes our grip.

We can start with Plato, writing about his teacher, Socrates, at the beginning of the fourth century BCE. Socrates appears as a character in a series of Platonic dialogues, known for his irony, sharp wit, and paradoxical views. One of his more notorious doctrines is that "no one goes willingly toward the bad or what he believes to be bad . . . instead of to the good."[17] What the Greeks called "*akrasia*" is action undertaken, freely and intentionally, against one's better judgment, deliberately doing what one thinks is worse. According to Socrates, this is simply impossible. A shocking claim! It is, on the face of it, dispiritingly common to fall short of acting as one thinks one should. But the realists who insist on this still typically concede that it is *irrational* to choose against one's better judgment. When I smoke another cigarette, thinking I should quit, I am acting against reason.

It is natural to extend this thought to preference and desire. While it is possible to want what you think is bad, not to want what you think is good, and to prefer what you think is worse, these attitudes are thoroughly irrational. But then Adams must be wrong. Our lawyer believes she should have persisted with piano when she could. Her life as a lawyer is no better than expected.

Nor can she point to the existence of a child as a reason to affirm her past mistake. Yet if she follows Adams's pattern, she is glad she did not decide on music, even as she grants that her actual decision was worse. Socrates is rolling in his grave.

In the last few decades, behavioral economists have pushed back on the injunction to pursue the best. In the strategy of "satisficing"—named by Herbert Simon in 1956[18]—we settle for outcomes that are good enough, and do not fret about the fact that others are surely better. This is one way to cope with the excess of options characteristic of modern life.[19] Buying a new shirt, the satisficer stops when he has one that fits well, looks good, and is not overpriced. The maximizer keeps shopping, since other shirts may be cheaper and more stylish. What about the cost in time? He factors that in, too: another dimension to be weighed and optimized. So much work!

Satisficing may be sound policy, but it doesn't vindicate the life-affirming lawyer. It is one thing to say, "I know there are better options, but I am not going to search for them, since this one is good enough." It is quite another to say, "I know a specific option that is better than this one, but I don't want it." The first remark makes sense, but it is the second that is relevant here. Nat believes that a specific option, trying to succeed as a pianist, was better than the one she took. She should have chosen it back then. But she does not prefer it now.

Nor can we explain how her attitude shifts. If satisficing is rational, Nat could do it in advance, defending her decision from the start: "Law is good enough for me; why bother with music?" That is not what happens. Instead, Nat ends up being glad she made a choice that she regards as a mistake.

Perhaps she came around in the wake of her decision, only then beginning to satisfice? But even this falls short. The most we get from satisficing is indifference to the better option, not an active desire for something else, as for law over music. There may be no point crying over spilled milk; that doesn't mean one should be happy that the milk was spilled.

We are beginning to see the trouble with Adams's insight. What he is advocating is an unprecedented split between comparative assessment and desire: preferring what you think is worse. If that is not irrational, what is?

In the case of procreation, we have something to say: "Yes, I should have waited to conceive. That would have been a wiser choice, and things have turned out as I thought they would. But the circumstance has changed. The actual existence of my son, who would not have existed otherwise, makes all the difference." It is much less credible to make this speech about activities or things. On a picture whose influence transcends philosophy—it belongs to the liberal humanist inheritance of Western culture—being irreplaceable is what distinguishes the value of human life from the value of anything else. Immanuel Kant, whose program we reviewed in chapter 1, contrasted dignity with price. "What has a price can be replaced with something else, as its *equivalent*," he wrote, "whereas, what is elevated above any price, and hence allows of no equivalent, has a dignity."[20] It is the dignity of human life that explains why you should not prefer to rewind time, erase your son, and try again. But a mere artifact, even a masterpiece like *Orlando*, has a price—in the Kantian sense, if not in U.S. dollars. If Woolf could have written a better novel, it seems irrational not to wish she had.

This point is, if anything, even clearer when it comes to things we do. Some thirty years ago, philosopher Michael Bratman noted that, while projects place demands on us—you have to finish what you have started—the mere adoption of a project does not provide additional reason for its pursuit.[21] We could otherwise justify bad decisions simply by making them, which is absurd. To take a mundane example, suppose I am back in graduate school, deciding on a class for the spring semester. I can either take logic, which will benefit my work but which I find more difficult, or a class in ethics, which I know I will enjoy but from which I will learn much less. It's a very close call. In the end, carefully weighing the pros and cons, I conclude that logic makes more sense. That is what I should take. Unfortunately, *akrasia* strikes! Daunted by the forest of symbols, I sign up for ethics, against my better judgment. If the actual existence of a project were a reason for affirmation, like the existence of a child, I could now point to the fact that I am taking ethics as a reason to affirm my choice, embracing it in retrospect: "I made a mistake, but I am glad I did, since if I had chosen otherwise, this activity would not exist." That seems quite wrong. As with artifacts, so with projects: their value is not dignity, but price. There is no reason to prefer what I am actually doing to alternatives that would have been better, just because I am doing it.

The case of relationships is trickier. Lovers do not "trade up," dropping one another when the prospect of a better relationship comes along. But if you truly believe that you would have had a better marriage with X than Y, and Y would have been just fine, shouldn't you wish it had been you and X all along? It may be too late, now, but that is no reason to dismiss a retroactive romance.

The upshot is that we are very much in the dark about the wisdom of Adams's idea. It is inspiring to be told we can affirm our lives exactly as they are, that the existence of these activities, artifacts, relationships has the power to redeem the past, quieting regret. But it sounds too good to be true.

IS IGNORANCE BLISS?

Let me try to shed some light.

At least two paths remain to be explored. One goes deeper than the other, but they are both instructive in their way. According to the first, the pivotal feature of retrospection is that, when you look back on your life, it is given to you, free of risk. Your life so far lies in the past, and there is little or no uncertainty in how it all turned out. The desire to rewrite history, by contrast, is the desire to take a chance, the chance of something better. Whether it is rational to want that now depends on the rationality of being averse to risk, preferring a bird in the hand to two in the bush. In this respect, your situation is very different from the one you faced in prospect, when there were risks to be encountered either way.

Think about Nat, deciding between music and law. In the jargon of economists, Nat is mildly risk averse. She is willing to gamble a bit, but not too much. Suppose she is asked to choose between two bets: ticket A pays forty dollars if a coin comes up heads, ten dollars if it comes up tails; ticket B pays a hundred dollars for heads, nothing for tails. Nat would choose ticket B and she thinks it is irrational not to. (The "expected value" of ticket A, the value of the payoffs discounted by probability, is twenty-five dollars; the expected value of ticket B is fifty.) On the other hand, if she had to choose between ticket B and forty dollars in the hand, she would refuse to gamble. She thinks that's sensible, too.

What has this got to do with major life decisions? The point is that, from Nat's perspective, law is like ticket A, a gamble with a low ceiling but a fairly high floor. Things may go better or worse, but she will likely end up in a job with decent pay and have a reasonable quality of life. Music is ticket B, with a higher ceiling but a lower floor. Although Nat loves piano, there is a greater chance of disappointment and professional failure, years of frustration and heartbreak, with little to show for them. On balance, Nat believes that she should take the risk. It is better to gamble on music than law. But she doesn't follow through. Instead, she applies to law school, choosing the equivalent of ticket A, and the rest is history.

Looking back, her situation has changed. Life as a lawyer has turned out fine. Nat doesn't hate her job, and it pays well; she has her husband, Al, her friends, hobbies, vacations. Among the range of outcomes she anticipated, this is pretty good, closer to forty than ten. Nat still believes she made a bad decision when she quit piano, choosing ticket A over ticket B. But the question of regret is different. Would she now give up her life as a successful lawyer for a gamble she cannot predict? The answer may well be no. In retrospect, Nat is comparing ticket B—a hundred for heads but nothing for tails—with forty dollars in the hand. It is perfectly rational to refuse that risk.

The mechanism here is not unlike the one that draws on unexpected outcomes, as in the unfortunate plane crash and my bizarre epiphany. But it needn't turn on false beliefs, miscalculations, or factual errors. As I have told the story, Nat may have been exactly right about the probabilities and payoffs. But there is still the matter of chance: uncertainty and risk in how things will turn out. If it is rational to be risk averse, to prefer good things you know to the uncertain prospect of better ones, it can be rational to prefer in retrospect decisions you should not have made.

In order to use this procedure in cognitive therapy, you will have to ask yourself how risk averse you ought to be. That is a personal question. But we can formulate rules of thumb. First, when you reflect on past mistakes or on events you did not welcome at the time, asking, "Do I wish it hadn't happened?", do not fantasize about the best-case scenario, the hundred-dollar win. Remind yourself that the consequences were uncertain and that a second chance could turn out better or worse. Second, focus on the bird in hand. You know, more or less, how things worked out, and it is this specific past you are now comparing with a roll of the dice. So long as your actual life is good enough, and you are sufficiently risk averse, it is perfectly rational to be content with how things are, even though they could have been much better, and even though you still believe that they went wrong.

This is where we will leave our wistful lawyer, reconciled to her job and to what is, in the end, a pretty enviable life. The strategy of risk aversion works for her, and it may work for you. But it only goes so far. For one thing, it is silent when the missed alternative does not involve much risk or when its floor is very high. Even in retrospect, the gamble may look better than what you have. For another, appeal to risk is dismayingly negative, a source of resignation not delight. Can we make a more positive case for the affirmation of life? I think we can.

Begin with a moment of retrospection. Remember when I told you of the lives I haven't lived, my dreams of poetry and medicine. Remember the feeling of loss, even as I claimed, insisted, urged, that committing to philosophy made sense. And imagine, if you will, that I could not admit the truth. In fact, I knew I ought to be

a doctor, that for me it was a better choice, more meaningful, less selfish. But acting on a spiteful urge to disap-
point my father, who wanted me to be a doctor like him,
I picked the option he would least approve. Against my
better judgment, I took up philosophy and embarked
on a course I could not correct. I don't dislike my life—
far from it—but I do think that, in this respect, I made a
mistake. Am I compelled to regret it, still?

Searching through the tactics we have unearthed, I
could appeal to procreation: I would not have met my
wife, and my son would not exist, if I had become a doctor. But we can amend the story to rule this out. In the narrative we are now composing, I am childless, and I do not
want a child. (This is a work of fiction: any resemblance to
real persons, living or dead, is purely coincidental.) Nor
can I profess some startling revelation, finding philosophy
more worthwhile than I had hoped. I still believe it is a
worse career than being a doctor; I haven't changed my
mind. And though things have gone well for me, I am not
sufficiently risk averse to think it would be a mistake to
gamble on medicine when the alternative is as good as my
actual life. The result is that is nothing we have said so far
can help me. And yet I do not regret my past.

The explanation owes its shape to a final callback, this
time to the end of chapter 3, where I was sheltered by
ignorance from the ache of unsatisfied desire. Before I
made the choice of philosophy, setting poetry and medicine aside, I knew I could not have it all. But I did not
know what I would be missing. This made the fact of loss

much easier to bear. It is when I make the decision, when I know not just that there are deficits to come, but what those deficits are, that I am forced to confront what I will not do. And that is when it hurts. The explanation of this shift is epistemic: it has to do with knowledge. There is an emotional barrier between knowing that I will miss out on activities I value and knowing which ones.

This fact about distress has a constructive counterpart. Not only can ignorance protect us from the emotional impact of what is bad, knowledge can amplify the impact of what is good. There is a difference between knowing that something is worthwhile and knowing what makes it so, between knowing the existence of reasons for desire and knowing what those reasons are. Just as it is rational to respond less strongly to the abstract knowledge that your life will have deficiencies than to learning which ones, so it is rational to respond more strongly to the definite ways in which a life is good than to the nebulous fact that another life is better.

In our fiction, I am right to believe that I should have gone for medicine. But I know very little of what that would involve. I can say schematically that, had I been a doctor, I would have pulled long hours as a medical resident; I would have saved lives and lost them, too; I would have tried to care for patients with compassion as well as clinical skill. But there are deep limits to my comprehension. I believe I would have lived a better life in medicine, but I am ignorant of its texture, the enveloping substance of the work that makes it so worthwhile.

I know much more, inexpressibly more, about philosophy. I know students who feel they have had their own ideas for the very first time, their first glimpse of enlightenment, in conversation with Derek Parfit or David Hume. I cannot take credit, but I was there. I know that there is value in the history of philosophy, not in abstraction but through countless stories of intellectual and human drama—stories like that of John Stuart Mill—each one a reason to care that this knowledge is preserved. I see, if only through a haze, what Iris Murdoch meant when she wrote, "To do philosophy is to explore one's own temperament, and yet at the same time to attempt to discover the truth."[22] None of this can be conveyed effectively in a paragraph, an essay, a book, even by the poet I might have been.

The same thing can be said for you. It is a bleak life in which the attempt to describe what is good, the moments that matter, the close relationships, the intricate fabric of days and weeks and years, would not eclipse what you could say in a million words. (This is true even if the bad things, too, have texture, and the words for them are endless.)

This is what I place against the fact that I should have been a doctor: not the inarticulate claim that my life is not so bad but a litany of reasons to affirm it, reasons I cannot catalogue or contain. I know that if I had gone for medicine, my life would be as rich, and I believe its riches count for more than my actual life. But I do not know what they are. And what engages me, what grips my desire, shapes my preference, is not just better and worse, but all the distinctive, particular ways in which life has been good so far.

We live in details, not abstractions. If it is rational to respond more strongly to the facts that make something good, in all their specificity, than to the featureless, generic fact that something else is better, it is rational to be glad that I made a choice—to be a philosopher, not a physician—that I still believe is worse. What saves me from regret is not aversion to risk, the birth of a child, or an underestimation of philosophy. It is the amplitude of life, its unfathomable particularity, like the fastidious excess of a peasant scene by Bruegel.

At the risk of impertinence, I offer this thought to Virginia Woolf. What she has, instead of children, is not the bare existence of *Orlando* but its words and sentences, images, contexts, vision, its expression of life, "a luminous halo, a semi-transparent envelope surrounding us from the beginning of consciousness to the end."[23] And I offer it to you.

Mistakes, misfortunes, failures: no one makes it to midlife without acquiring some of each. I am sure that you have yours. Some have been redeemed by risk aversion, kids, or luck. Others not so much. You may be tempted to take stock, to wrestle with the past. There is nothing wrong with that. But do not make a further mistake, the mistake of stepping back, abstracting from the details of your life, to ask what you should want. In abstracting, you discard a vital source of rational affirmation: not the bare existence of activities, artifacts, relationships, but their impossibly verdant depths. Do not weigh alternatives theoretically, but zoom in: let the specifics count against the grand cartoon of lives un-lived. In doing so, you may find you cannot regret what you should have resisted at the time.

I hope that this is true, but I make no promises. Not every wound can heal. In the face of "terrible, searing regret," you may be lucidly unconsoled. If so, I am sorry. It is easier to embrace the details as a kind of recompense when your mistakes hurt only you; much harder when they hurt someone else. "You can, of course, experiment with your own life," Jay concedes in Kureishi's *Intimacy*. "Maybe you shouldn't do it with other people's."[24] Despite its power, the tactic of attending to particulars can fail.

I'll end by marking one more risk. If part of what protects you from regret, or mutes its force, is an asymmetry of knowledge—your comparative ignorance of the lives you could have lived—your tranquility depends on its persistence. In order to avoid regret, you must preserve a measure of oblivion. There is a corresponding threat. The more you know what you are missing, the more you learn what the alternatives would have been and what they would involve, the harder it becomes to let them go. Hence a parting word to the retrospective: be careful what you study, where you choose to train your eye. A little knowledge is harmless; too much can tax your peace of mind. Do not obsess about the might-have-beens: "where ignorance is bliss, / 'Tis folly to be wise."[25]

5

SOMETHING TO LOOK FORWARD TO

The third volume of Simone de Beauvoir's autobiography ends with a passage some have found mystifying:

> I can still see the hedge of hazel trees flurried by the wind and the promises with which I fed my beating heart while I stood gazing at the gold mine at my feet: a whole life to live. The promises have all been kept. And yet, turning an incredulous gaze toward that young and credulous girl, I realize with stupor how much I have been swindled.[1]

This is the final sentence of the book.

An iconic feminist thinker and sometime partner of Jean-Paul Sartre, Beauvoir might have found many reasons for complaint. Were the promises deformed by oppressive ideals of femininity? As she wrote in *The Second Sex*, "One is not born, but rather becomes, a woman."[2] Gender is a cultural construction, and it wasn't built for the benefit of women. Did she have too limited a view of what was possible for her, doubting her philosophical gifts in the intimidating but inspiring presence of Sartre?[3]

Perhaps, but at least by her own account, she had something else in mind. Pressed to clarify her conclusion in the *Paris Review*, Beauvoir had this to say:

People . . . have tried to interpret [the final sentence] to mean that my life has been a failure, either because I recognize the fact that I was mistaken on a political level or because I recognize that after all a woman should have had children, etc. Anyone who reads my book carefully can see that I say the very opposite, that I don't envy anyone, that I'm perfectly satisfied with what my life has been, that I've kept all my promises and that consequently if I had my life to live over again I wouldn't live it any differently.[4]

Not mistakes or failures or missing out: Beauvoir could skip the last two chapters of this book. But in the heart of middle age, at fifty-five, she felt herself imprisoned by the inexorable passage of time.

When one has an existentialist view of the world, like mine, the paradox of human life is precisely that one tries to *be* and, in the long run, merely exists. It's because of this discrepancy that when you've laid your stake on being—and, in a way you always do when you make plans, even if you actually know that you can't succeed in being—when you turn around and look back on your life, you see that you've simply existed. In other words, life isn't behind you like a solid thing, like the life of a god (as it is conceived, that is, as something impossible). Your life is simply a human life.[5]

A god's activities may be timeless. For us, the living present fades into lifeless past, and in the end takes each of us with it. Beauvoir connects her dismay at non-being with the prospect of inevitable death: "I think with sadness of all the books I've read, all the places I've seen, all the knowledge I've amassed and that will be no more. All the music, all the paintings, all the culture, so many places: and suddenly nothing."[6]

We have been putting this off too long. It is time to face our own mortality. In the essay that got us started, Elliott Jaques called this "the central and crucial feature of the mid-life phase—the feature which precipitates the critical nature of the period."[7] "The paradox is that of entering the prime of life, the stage of fulfilment, but at the same time the prime and fulfilment are dated. Death lies beyond."[8] In middle age, the limited span of human life is no longer an abstraction. You know from the inside what a decade means; those that remain to you can be counted on one hand. That can be a source of angst.

The idea that philosophy will console us in our mortality is an old one. When essayist Michel de Montaigne wrote, in 1580, "To philosophize is to learn how to die,"[9] he was joining a tradition that went back through Roman philosopher Cicero in the first century BCE all the way to Socrates, drinking hemlock in an Athenian prison. Montaigne's philosophical turn was caused in part by the death of his closest friend, Étienne de la Boétie, in part by a riding accident in which he himself was nearly killed. Étienne was thirty-three; Michel was thirty-six. Montaigne went on to perform a legendary feat of self-exploration, writing the 500,000 words of his humane, inquiring *Essays*, whose topics range from cannibalism, to pedantry, to the human thumb. But his philosophizing ends in failure. "If you do not know how to die, never mind," he urges ruefully in his penultimate essay, "Nature will tell you how to do it on the spot"[10]—the implication being that only death will silence the electric, halting terror that the thought of death provokes.

I will try to do better, but I won't pretend it's easy. This chapter explores some philosophical attempts to wrestle with death. There will be blood, sweat, and tears; there will be insight and illusion. Progress will be difficult. From the standpoint of the cognitive therapist, death turns out to be a killer.

NOTHING TO US?

If Montaigne is a progenitor of this book, a cerebral self-help guide, Epicurus is even more so. A younger contemporary of Aristotle, Epicurus was both philosopher and lifestyle guru, presiding over an idyllic, secluded commune in ancient Athens dubbed "the Garden." Nowadays, "Epicurean" connotes a life of sensual pleasure:

wild parties and gourmet meals. If you had gone to the Garden in pursuit of that, you would have left frustrated. What Epicurus prized was "*ataraxia*," or tranquility and freedom from pain, achieved through abstemious contemplation in the quiet company of friends.

The greatest threat to happiness, he believed, was an extravagant fear of death, poisoning our peace of mind and troubling our days. No doubt the process of dying can be degrading and painful. It makes sense to hope for a quiet end. But dying is not the same as being dead. For Epicurus, death is the permanent end of our existence: no survival as a disembodied soul, no afterlife, no second chance. (I will follow him in this; the challenge of facing death looks very different if it is a matter of uncertainty what happens when we die, with the prospect of reincarnation or eternity in heaven or hell.) It is fear of being dead that Epicurus finds both prevalent and irrational. Paradoxically, it is the fact of nonexistence that gives solace, abolishing mortal fear. "So death, the most terrifying of ills, is nothing to us," he wrote, "since so long as we exist, death is not with us; but when death comes, then we do not exist. It does not then concern either the living or the dead, since for the former it is not, and the latter are no more."[11]

I don't know about you, but I find this pretty cold comfort. I was shocked to see the argument repeated, without criticism, in a popular book of "existential psychotherapy," Irvin Yalom's *Staring at the Sun*.[12] If it works for you, fine; stop reading here. (A philosophical spoiler alert.) For those still with me: I am sorry to say that the argument is not sound. From the premise that you won't exist when you die, it follows that being dead cannot involve the positive harm of suffering. It can still involve the harm of deprivation: the permanent cessation of everything good in life. No more art, no more knowledge, no more time with friends, nothing. What could make more sense than to treat this prospect with dread, as you would a drab, insipid future, joyless but free from pain? A grim occupation.

The idea that ceasing to exist is bad for us because it deprives us of benefits has some claim to orthodoxy: it is the overwhelmingly common response to Epicurus among contemporary philosophers. The misfortune of being dead is the misfortune of an absence, a lack, a void of whatever it is that makes life worth living. In terms we used to diagnose Mill's nervous breakdown, it is a loss of existential value, the kind of value that is not just ameliorative—solving problems and fulfilling needs—but makes life positively good. If our activities had only ameliorative worth, Epicurus would have a point. The best we could hope for in life would be freedom from suffering, which death would then provide. But it is our blessing and our curse that life can be much more than that. Following the second rule in chapter 2, we pursue activities whose value is existential, ensuring that, if things go well, it is good to be alive.

Defenders of Epicurus—they do exist—sometimes complain that we are missing his point. He is not denying that death is worse than a continued life of worthwhile activity, but asking what attitude we should take to this reality. It might be argued, for instance, that *fear* of death is inappropriate, since it only makes sense to fear what threatens positive harm, or what is in some way uncertain. Since death is certain deprivation, it is irrational to fear it. As it stands, this is the kind of pedantry that gives philosophers a bad name. It doesn't matter if you call it "fear" or "dread" or "sadness": what counts is the profound aversion many of us experience in the face of death. Epicurus cannot win on a technicality. But there is more going on. We saw in chapter 4 that rational preference can diverge from what is better and worse. Something similar might hold for death. However bad it may be to die, we should not quake at mortality. So say the followers of Epicurus, including his most influential convert, Titus Lucretius Carus, a contemporary of Cicero in ancient Rome. We inherit from Lucretius a beguiling image of death on which it is, as it was for Epicurus, nothing to fear. Can this be put to therapeutic use?

MAN IN THE MIRROR

About Lucretius himself we know very little. Centuries later, St. Jerome would allege that he went insane while writing his philosophical poem, *De Rerum Natura*—"on the nature of things"—having imbibed a potent aphrodisiac; Lucretius went on to kill himself at forty-four. Not surprisingly, scholars have expressed doubts about the depiction of a pagan philosopher as a lovesick madman by a Christian saint.[13] The work itself was lost for a thousand years. Rediscovered in a German monastery in 1417, it became a founding text of the Italian Renaissance.

As the name of his poem suggests, Lucretius covers a lot of ground: in essence, all of it. The bit that matters to us is a metaphor whose impact far exceeds its throwaway feel. Echoing Epicurus, Lucretius aims to reshape our relationship with death.

> Look back now and consider how the bygone ages of eternity that elapsed before our birth were nothing to us. Here, then, is a mirror in which nature shows us the time to come after our death. Do you see anything fearful in it? Do you perceive anything grim? Does it not appear more peaceful than the deepest sleep?[14]

Lucretius does not return to this image, which may present no more than the standard Epicurean view: we cannot be harmed by the deprivation of benefits we are not there to receive. (See the spoiler above.) But it has taken on a life of its own, its reflections visible outside philosophy, as when Vladimir Nabokov depicts human life as "a brief crack of light between two eternities of darkness" in the opening lines of *Speak, Memory*.[15] In philosophy, it is the source of a puzzle about death that is known as the "symmetry argument" but is more aptly posed as a question: What, if anything, makes it rational to respond so differently to postmortem and prenatal nonexistence, the one a source of paralyzed anxiety, the other blank indifference? The challenge is to explain and justify contrasting attitudes to phenomena that are, in themselves, identical.

Not everyone feels the contrast quite so vividly. When my son, Eli, had just turned four, we visited the in-laws and I showed him a baby picture of my wife. The following dialogue ensued.

> E: This is mommy when she was a baby.
>   Was I a baby then?
> K: No, you weren't born yet.
> E: Was I a grown-up or a mommy?
> K: No, you weren't anyone.
> E: That's sad, not being anyone.

For Eli, not having existed conjures sadness, not indifference. While his verdict on mortality may be darker, as far as I can tell I have not passed on to him my frantic aversion to the looming void. If I had, he might resemble the "chronophobiac" reported by Nabokov, who experiences panic on seeing a home video of the world before he was born, a world without him.[16]

The symmetry argument assumes a more conventional attitude to prenatal nonexistence and tries to induce a similar equanimity toward death. It is essential to the force of this approach that we see past more trivial differences between the time after death and the time before

111

conception or birth. For one thing, if I were not to die in year N, but ten years later, I would live a longer life, and if things go well, enjoy more benefits. In contrast, if I had been born in 1966, not ten years later, there is no reason to think my longevity would increase. (Actuarial numbers suggest the opposite.) There is a mundane reason to wish for later death, not for earlier birth: that way, you get more years of life. For another thing, if I had been born in 1966, my life would have been dramatically different. It is hard to know how it would have gone. The pressures explored at the end of chapter 4, both risk aversion and attention to particulars, speak against this option, even if we stipulate that it brings another decade of well-being.

These points are fair, but they are superficial. They don't get close to the depth of felt divergence between finitude in the road ahead and in the rearview mirror. Many of us are plagued by a longing for indefinite extension of life into the future, for life without end. The desire for indefinite extension of life into the past, for life without origin, is at best eccentric, an amusing quirk, at worst pathological: Nabokov's chronophobia. (Imagine someone wishing that instead of being born, they had always existed, remembering episodes through the history of time, but facing death in the next fifty years.) This contrast is not explained by some disparity in duration between infinite future and infinite past, or by the rational impact of knowing what is good about one's actual life when the alternative is better.

For the advocate of symmetry, it is not explained, or justified, by anything. Prenatal nonexistence may be a terrible deprivation, much worse than infinite life, but it is not reasonable to react to it with more than mild dismay. Unless we can argue otherwise, that should also be our attitude to death. Postmortem nonexistence: a terrible deprivation, much worse than infinite life, but the object of only mild dismay. In principle, one could achieve parity by going the other way, inflating one's aversion to prenatal nonexistence, adding chronophobia to chronic fear of death. In practice, there is little threat of that. At worst, one's attitude might become what I hope is Eli's: a resigned melancholy about the time before one came to be, one's retrospective finitude, as about one's prospective annihilation.

We have found our first respectable therapy for those who are gripped by fear of death, also cited, this time more credibly, by Irvin Yalom.[17] Its efficacy does not rest on any mistake. But it is precarious. It turns on the conviction that there is no relevant contrast between prenatal and postmortem nonexistence, nothing to break the rational symmetry in which one is a mere reflection of the other. How safe is that assumption?

Enter Derek Parfit, whom we met in chapter 4, musing on the limits of regret. Eight years later, Parfit turned his attentive eye to an undeniable contrast between the time before birth and the time after death, whatever their intrinsic similarity: one is in the past, while the other is yet to come. Do our opposing temporal orientations to prenatal and postmortem nonexistence make it rational to be more averse to one than to the other? Parfit's view is appropriately subtle: our desires may respond to the direction of time, treating past and future differently— but perhaps they should not.

Parfit illustrates his stance with another famous thought experiment, the story of My Past or Future Operations.[18] An abbreviated version:

> You wake up in hospital, knowing you had to go in for a vital procedure but not sure whether or not it has taken place. The nurse can't remember either: you might be the patient who had the operation yesterday, performed without anesthetic, lasting four painful hours; or you might be scheduled to have the procedure later today, again without anesthetic, but less onerous, lasting just one hour. She will look at the chart and let you know.

Parfit asks: What news are you hoping to receive? His guess, and mine, is that you hope you had the procedure done yesterday, even though your life will then include more hours of pain. We are, as Parfit argues, "biased towards the future": more concerned about pain we have yet to suffer than pain we have suffered in the past.[19] The same is true, in reverse, for pleasure. If you have been looking forward to a fun experience—going to a party, say—and you are unsure whether it happened yesterday or is scheduled for tonight, most likely you are hoping

for the latter. Future pleasures count for more than pleasures in the past. (In order to abstract from the pleasures
of recollection, which tend to blur the lines, we can stipulate that you won't remember the party, whenever it
takes place. It is that kind of party.)

If you are biased toward the future, you will not be
impressed by the "symmetry" of prenatal and postmortem nonexistence.[20] You will refuse the consolation offered above. While future finitude robs you of future
pleasures, which you deeply desire, past finitude robs
you of past ones, a matter of comparative indifference.
No wonder death inspires dread, unlike the bygone ages
of eternity.

We can read future bias back into Beauvoir's stupor.
No matter what pleasures you promise yourself, when
the promises are kept, the pleasures are no more. They
seem in retrospect to count for nothing, or at least for
less than they did in prospect, gazing at the gold mine
at your feet. We are inevitably swindled.

As Parfit would insist, however, the fact that you are
future-biased, if you are, does not settle the decisive question, whether your attitude is ultimately rational. It explains how you feel, but may not justify it. Parfit contends
that we should give up future bias, though it can't be said
that he presents a proof. One of his main points on behalf
of "temporal neutrality"—giving equal weight to experiences past and future—is that it mitigates fear of death.[21]

It is fair to say, I think, that the rationality of future
bias is an unsolved problem in philosophy. On the one

hand, it is hard to believe that the common response to My Past or Future Operations is irrational. On the other hand, it leads fairly rapidly to peculiar results. Imagine being asked, a week before the operation is scheduled, whether you prefer to have four hours of painful surgery on Monday morning or one hour on Tuesday afternoon. It's up to you. Unless you are quite unusual, you will opt for Tuesday. If you are future-biased, however, we can predict with confidence that, as you wake on Tuesday morning, you will regret your choice. At that point, you are in Parfit's scenario, wishing for the four-hour procedure on Monday over one hour later today. If future bias is rational, it is rational to make decisions you know for sure you are going to regret. Can that possibly be right?

I leave that question to you, stuck in the middle of things, with forty-odd years behind you and, if all goes well, a similar span ahead. Can you adopt an attitude of temporal neutrality, on which death is a mirror of prenatal nonexistence? As life passes, "[you] have less and less to look forward to, but more and more to look backward to."[22] And that is just as good. If you can manage it without lapsing into chronophobia, you will have gone a long way toward acceptance of mortality, with philosophical help.

But I have to confess. As you can likely tell from the conditional mode of the last few pages, it doesn't work for me. I don't object to temporal neutrality, and I acknowledge the upsides, but I think it is reasonable to be future-biased, too. Temperamentally, I am closer to Beauvoir than Parfit, closer to resentment at time's implacable flow than to appreciation of the durable reality of the past. When I look in the mirror, I see a man who is biased toward the future, and whose fear of death remains profound. Is there nothing we can say to him?

TOO MUCH OF A GOOD THING?

Forget future bias for a moment and consider, directly, the desire not to die, a desire expressed with unforgettable verve by philosopher Miguel de Unamuno: "I do not want to die. No! I do not want to die, and I do not want to want to die. I want to live always, forever and ever."[23] As this brings out, the desire not to die amounts to a desire for eternal life. This prompts a therapeutic angle. If we could persuade ourselves that immortality is undesirable, we might be reconciled to death.

Philosophers have spilled considerable ink alleging that immortal life is not what it's cracked up to be. According to British philosopher Bernard Williams, the threat of immortality is boredom: bitter, excruciating, hopeless—not the kind that gives way to constant bliss.[24] According to Americans Martha Nussbaum and Samuel Scheffler, the problem is alienation.[25] Eternal life would be so radically different from the human condition that it would not sustain the activities that give meaning to our mortal days. Nor is it just philosophers who have it in for immortality. From withered Tithonus, the mythic Greek who was granted immortality but not eternal youth, to the nomadic, exiled family of Natalie Babbitt's children's classic, *Tuck Everlasting*, almost every novel, play, or film about living forever is a dystopia. Beauvoir wrote one of these herself: *All Men Are Mortal*, in which the struggles of a disaffected actress are set against the meaningless days of immortal aristocrat Raymond Fosca.

This deluge of critique is either a symptom of our deep need for mortality or a desperate attempt to conceal the truth. I won't attempt to settle which, though I have my suspicions. For there is a more prosaic retort to the desperate hunger for eternity. However wonderful it might be to live forever, isn't there something disproportionate in a painful longing for what is humanly impossible, in mourning one's mortality as if it were a grave misfortune, rather than the absence of a superpower? It makes sense to grieve a terminal diagnosis, a condition that will prevent you from living a full human life. And it could make sense to wish for immortality. But is it rational to quake at the frustration of that desire?

A friend shares his love of Superman and the wish that he too could be "Faster than a speeding bullet, more powerful than a locomotive, able to leap tall buildings in a single bound." Makes sense to me: who wouldn't want that? But when I see him months later, he looks terrible. He has been waking in a cold sweat, angst-ridden, bitter at the fact that he cannot fire laser beams from his eyes, railing at his merely human, not Kryptonian powers. He needs to get a grip! It is no misfortune to lack capacities that exceed the range of human possibility, not something that should fill you with despair.

How is the desire for immortality different? Even if being immortal is a very great good, it is like the ability to fly: a magical quality whose absence it is perverse to mourn. We may resent the threat of dying at forty-five. But if death comes at the end of the human span, at eighty-five or ninety, should it provoke our rage? We have had our allotment of years, and while we may want more, to insist on them looks like avarice: a shameless, pathological lust for life. This accusation could be made against Beauvoir, complaining that her life is not "the life of a god," one of enduring presence, but "is simply a human life," subject to the passage of time.[26] It is one thing to dream of living as a timeless deity, another to feel swindled by the fact that this is just a dream. Seen in this light, Beauvoir's angst at mortality is excessive, an expression of greed, an intemperate demand for superhuman powers.

Let us reflect on immortality as a radical change in the human condition, akin to growing wings or reproducing by fission; let us meditate on the difference between things it is rational to want and ones whose lack we should resent or grieve. In my admittedly unscientific studies, the practice of doing so can make the prospect of mortality less awful. If nothing else, we can try to shame ourselves for the intensity of our desire to live forever, adding insult to the injury of death.

I am the last person to miss an opportunity for self-reproach, but I am afraid that here too, consolation has its limits. (I hope I can admit this without endangering any progress you have made.) The fundamental limitation of this second therapy is that it treats the desire for immortality as a matter of wanting the best for oneself, in this case the *very* best, a benefit that goes beyond what is humanly possible. It is wrong to be possessed by this voracious and acquisitive urge. But this is not the only source of fear or dread in the face of death, and other sources are less readily tamed. Along with self-interest, there is self-preservation: two motives that are not the same.

One way to distinguish them is to look at a phenomenon that has been neglected in philosophy but is central to our relationship with mortality at midlife: the experience of bereavement and loss. It is in middle age, more often than not, that death becomes less abstract, not a crest on the horizon but a wave that crashes through your life, swallowing people you love. You are forced to watch them drown. Philosophers tend to think about death in the first person, but it is not a coincidence that some of the most profound confrontations with death begin with the death of a friend. Thus Gilgamesh begins his quest for immortality in the earliest surviving work of literature, dating from 2100 BCE:

Gilgamesh wept over Enkidu his friend,
bitterly he wept through the wilderness.
"Must I die too? Must I be as lifeless
as Enkidu? How can I bear this sorrow

that gnaws at my belly, this fear of death
that restlessly drives me onward? . . ."[27]

For many, it is the death of a parent that brings mortality close to home.

Let me risk some armchair psychology. When a loved one dies, we recoil for more than one reason. There is the thought of death as depriving them of life: a serious harm, especially when death is premature. Loving them, we wish them well, and so we want them not to die. But there is a second reaction, too: a distinct, primitive desire that they continue to be. This is not about well-being but about loss, the loss of someone who counts. Loving them, we are attached to them, and we don't want to let go.

Love has at least two sides: concern for another's well-being, wanting the best for them; and the perception of a value worth preserving, a passionate response to the dignity of human life. When you love someone, you see that their existence matters, that they cannot be replaced. (Here I echo, again, the Kantian contrast between dignity and price, which we encountered in chapter 4.) These dimensions can conflict with one another. If someone you love is suffering without hope of recovery, in palliative care, they may have nothing to gain from going on. Even as you admit this, wishing for their sake that the end is not far off, there is a counterforce to overcome, the force of loving attachment. At some level, you don't want their light to be extinguished, even though

121

their time has come. It takes work to accept what you know is for the best.

So, at least, it seems to me. (I grant that here, perhaps more than anywhere, one should mistrust generalizations.) If my depiction resonates with you, you will be able to separate two things: wanting the best for those you love and wanting them to stay alive. Although I have called it "attachment," the second desire need not be selfish, a desire not to lose someone; it is the desire that they not be lost. When I think about my son dying, I hope long after I am gone, I picture him as an old man, wizened, slowed, exhausted. And I suffer the same aversion. What hurts is not the end of our relationship—too late for that—but Eli's ceasing to be. This vicarious wish for immortality is not a matter of wanting the best for him, but a distinct expression of love.

And then there is love for oneself. Rather than starting from the inside, facing death, with the loss of those we love a shadow of our own mortality, we should approach death from the outside, taking bereavement as a model of what to feel. There is more than one source of grief about the fact that I will die. I want the best for myself: if immortality would be an infinite good, I am bound to be let down. But I have a further, primitive desire for my own persistence, an attachment to myself that is not concern for my well-being, but an intimate awareness of value, the dignity I share with every human soul.

The problem with our second therapy, its ultimate shortcoming, is that it speaks to one desire but not the other. Where the urge for immortality is a function of wanting the best for oneself, it is akin to wishing for a superpower: perfectly rational, in its way, but not a sensible ground of bitterness or grief. It is a form of avarice to suffer at the fact that your wish will not be granted. But moderating this desire is not enough to make peace with death. For there remains, untouched, the sense of irreplaceability, wanting yourself to endure as you do the people you love. There is no intemperance in recoiling from extinction in the wake of this desire, irrespective of what is good for you. So, again, our therapy is partial. Its efficacy depends on why you are averse to death, what troubles you about it: the deprivation of benefits or the bare cessation of life?

At the same time, something is gained by seeing one's death reflected in that of others, in picturing mortality as bereavement. We are reminded to proportion our demands on life to human scale, and to acknowledge that, however painful it may be, there is a process of accepting death, even the death of those you love, even when the loved one is you. It may feel impossible now, but in weathering the death of a parent or a friend, you can learn to let go—as you and I will one day have to let go of ourselves. If we can do it now, so much the better.

THE BITTER END

This is a difficult chapter to conclude. If only from self-interest, I had hoped to show that fear of death is misconceived, that philosophy will cure the grief of being mortal—not by cheating death, but by finding some confusion in the boundless desire to live. It hasn't turned out that way. When I lie sleepless, thinking of the final moments of my life, the final look, the final touch, the final taste, stunned by panic, I am not making a logical error. There is no refuting this despair, no conceptual distinction that will make it vanish: "This is a special way of being afraid / No trick dispels."[28] (Philip Larkin, again: the poet who invented sexual intercourse in 1963.)

But philosophy isn't nothing. Meditation on prenatal nonexistence, the nothing before us, is itself no different from the nothing to come: it helps those less prone to future bias. They can see death as the merely disappointing image of the prior abyss. Conceiving immortality as a superpower, an extravagant gift, not a sensible demand: it helps those whose love is more giving, wanting the best for themselves and others, less an impulse to preserve what matters, grief at the fragility of life. They can see excess in the desire to live forever.

My guess is that, if these therapies work for you, you were already less afraid of death than Larkin or me, more well-adjusted, not as prone to sleepless panic. I offer them, anyway. It would be a miserly physician who will not medicate others until he has healed himself. And this is not the end. Even for me, there is a whisper of hope in the idea that love is not one single thing, in distinguishing attachment from concern. I see that there is room for loving-kindness, wanting the best for someone, without being attached to them, unable to let go. There is a way to accept mortality in which there is no denial of life.

Here, I believe, the legacy of Cicero, Lucretius, and Montaigne, in Western philosophy, converges with a branch of Buddhist thought. Buddhism begins with the "Four Noble Truths," but their brevity is deceptive. The first three are one-liners: life is suffering; the source of suffering is attachment; the goal is to give it up. The fourth noble truth is an "Eightfold Path"—which rather defeats the arithmetic promise. (How many noble truths are there, in fact? Eleven? Or more, if some of the eight turn out to be more than one?) The Eightfold Path defeats complacency in another way, since it is not a truth one assimilates by intellect alone. It involves a sustained practice of purification through mindfulness. This is the point at which cognitive therapy fails: you can learn to live without attachment, but not by reading a book.

Unlike some Buddhists, I don't believe attachment is inevitably possessive. I don't think the vertigo I feel when I anticipate Eli's death is really about me. It is an intelligible response to the value I see in him, not an ethical mistake. All the same, there is insight in maintaining that attachment is not obligatory, that love is possible without it. There is a crack of light between two darknesses: avoidance of love and inescapable woe. That is where we should steer our ship.

The question is how. Here, too, there is an answer in the Buddhist tradition, though its ambition is sweeping and its efficacy unclear. In the final chapter of this book,

I will lead the way into Buddhist conceptions of mind-fulness through another confluence of East and West, a stream in Western thought that merges with the Eight-fold Path, though the waters are muddy and the currents mixed. I will breathe new life into a self-help cliché: "live in the present." I will plot a course through the depths of my own midlife crisis. And I will hazard observations on the lure of infidelity, early retirement, and the shiny sports car. If that is what you crave, your wait is almost at an end.

6
LIVING IN THE PRESENT

I am standing in my office at MIT, staring at the screen of my computer with my arms crossed, watching the cursor blink by the title, "Living in the Present," hesitating. Do I want to write this chapter?

Of course I do. I have been working on this book for months and thinking about it for years. I want to finish writing it. But to be perfectly honest, the thought of doing so fills me with dread. I put the question directly to myself, "Suppose that the book were finished, the prose revised and edited, the proofs returned: would this be a great joy and happiness to you?" And an irrepressible self-consciousness distinctly answers "No!" At best, I am ambivalent. When I finish this book, I will be glad to have done something I believe is worth doing, but I will have to say goodbye to a project that has meant a lot to me. That will leave a hole in my life.

If experience is anything to go by, the hole will be filled soon enough. There will be another project: a class to teach, a book to read, an article to write. I will move on. But the movement is like running on a treadmill. Life is a succession of projects, each one left behind, their numbers slowly adding up. What the future holds is only more of the achievements, and the failures, that make up my past. It will differ only in quantity from the life I have already lived, a mere accumulation of deeds.

It is not just work. There are the conventional milestones of personal life: first kiss, first girlfriend, losing my virginity, getting engaged, getting married, having kids, getting them through diapers, through high school, college, into lives of their own—what comedian Stewart Lee calls "the sheer interminable human joy of it all."[1] These accomplishments matter to me, but each one is bittersweet: longed for, pursued, and ultimately, disappointingly, complete. That's over with. What now?

The sense of repetition and futility, the emptiness of satisfied desire: I am not alone in feeling them. Maybe you have felt them, too, mired in the pursuits of middle age, one after the other, wondering what is next. We are textbook casualties of the midlife crisis, striving to achieve what seems worthwhile, succeeding well enough, yet at the same time restless and unfulfilled.

Despite the echo of Mill, my affliction does not respond to the treatment in chapter 2. The problem is not that writing a book or teaching a class has only ameliorative worth, like Mill's campaign of social reform, aimed at the reduction of human suffering. Whatever its utility in solving problems, meeting needs we would be better off without, philosophical endeavor goes beyond this: its value is existential. (So, at least, I believe, though it is not in this respect unique.)

Nor is the problem one of missing out (chapter 3) or going wrong (chapter 4): two modes of unsatisfied desire. The challenge is not frustration but getting what you want; the puzzle is that success can seem like failure. And whatever it may have to do with facing death—in my case, there is a deep association—the suspicion of something hollow in the sequence of accomplishments, chapters in the book of life, is not silenced by the prospect of eternity. Whatever is wrong with the pursuit of goal after worthy goal, it will not be cured by prolonging that pursuit forever.

We are circling a crisis more insidious than any we have confronted so far. Do not despair. Putting myself on the therapist's couch, coaxed by the obdurate philosopher, I will extract an account of my problem that is also its solution. The answer was in me all along. It was put there by Arthur Schopenhauer, the most notorious pessimist in the history of Western philosophy and a scrupulous critic of getting what you want.

WHAT SCHOPENHAUER GOT RIGHT

Schopenhauer was born in Danzig—now Gdansk, Poland—in 1788, the son of a merchant and a popular novelist. At fifteen, Arthur grudgingly agreed to drop his scholarly ambitions and take up the family business, as a condition of joining his parents on an enticing European tour.[2] It was a preposterously unfortunate decision. In the summer of 1803, Arthur witnessed executions in

London, saw fear and horror in the faces of men condemned; he visited public prisons in France, where criminals were displayed like animals in a zoo. Years later, he would compare his experience to the Buddha's formative encounter with sickness, old age, pain, and death: it was an indelible exposure to the wretchedness of human life.[3] Arthur's reward as an obedient son was, in short, the worst family vacation ever.

Matters did not improve. Two years later, his father died, drowned in a canal after falling from a warehouse loft in a suspected suicide.[4] Schopenhauer kept his promise to go into business. He survived two years of drudgery before returning to his studies, forced to move from Gotha to Göttingen to Berlin to Jena before finally earning his doctorate in 1813. His thesis, *On the Fourfold Root of the Principle of Sufficient Reason*, was dismissed by his mother, Johanna, as unreadable, a book "written for pharmacists" that no one would buy.[5] The tension between them did not abate. In 1814, Arthur moved to Dresden; he never set eyes on his mother again.

It was in Dresden that Schopenhauer wrote his masterpiece, *The World as Will and Representation*. Sadly, it was not recognized as a masterpiece right away. When Arthur was hired at the University of Berlin, he scheduled his lectures against those of Georg Wilhelm Friedrich Hegel, the most renowned philosopher of the day. It was like scheduling a TV pilot against the Superbowl. Predictably, no one came. Schopenhauer left Berlin, humiliated, in 1822. It was only at the end of his life that he achieved some measure of fame, for essays and reflections pub-lished in 1851 as *Parerga and Paralipomena* ("appendices" and "omissions"). He died nine years later, lying on the couch in his apartment, at the age of seventy-two.

You may not be surprised by Schopenhauer's mistrust of desire. But his position is unexpectedly severe: not that desires are too often frustrated but that they pose a di-lemma their satisfaction cannot solve. Suppose you do get what you want, your desire at last fulfilled. You should be delighted. Instead you are aimless and depressed. Your pursuit is over and you have nothing to do. Life needs direction. You must have desires, aims, projects that are as yet incomplete. And yet this, too, is fatal. For want-ing what you do not have is suffering. As Schopenhauer writes in *The World as Will and Representation*:

> The basis of all willing, however, is need, lack, and hence pain, and by its very nature and origin [the animal] is therefore destined to pain. If, on the other hand, it lacks objects of willing, because it is at once deprived of them again by too easy a satisfaction, a fearful emptiness and boredom comes over it; in other words, its being and its existence become an intolerable burden for it. Hence it swings like a pen-dulum to and fro between pain and boredom, and these two are in fact its ultimate constituents.[6]

This is Schopenhauer's dilemma. Either your will has objects or it doesn't: you want things or you don't. If you don't, you are aimless, and your life is empty. This is the abyss of boredom. Yet if you do have desires, they must be for outcomes so far unattained. These are the targets of your pursuit and thus of the activities that occupy your life. But it is painful to want what you do not have. In staving off boredom by finding things to do, you have condemned yourself to misery.

No wonder students did not flock to Schopenhauer's lectures: Arthur was the opposite of a motivational speaker. His picture of human life is inordinately bleak. It is true that life without goals is empty, if it counts as life at all. We need things to do and if we finish doing them, we need to find more. But the pursuit of goals is not pure agony. At least, it doesn't have to be. Wanting to write this book, I take a positive view of the future in which it is written and a negative view of the present, in which it is not: the draft sits incomplete on my computer's hard drive. For Schopenhauer, such negativity hurts. In fact, we may contend, it is not so bad. My attitude is one of interested preference, not urgent, agonized lust. To call this "suffering" is to give an exaggerated sense of the emotional impact of unsatisfied desire. Dilemma solved!

But Schopenhauer was on to something. There is insight in his cynical account of our relationship with desire. Think of it this way. What gives purpose to your life is having goals. Yet in pursuing them, you either fail (not good) or in succeeding, bring them to a close. If what you care about is achievement—earning a promotion, having a child, writing a book, saving a life—the completion of your project may be of value, but it means that the project can no longer be your guide. Sure, you have other goals, and you can formulate new ones. The problem is not the risk of running out, the aimless nightmare of Schopenhauer's boredom. It is that your engagement with value is self-destructive. The way in which you relate to the activities that matter most to you is by trying to complete them and so expel them from your life. Your days are devoted to ending, one by one, the activities that give them meaning. The fact that you cannot eliminate all of them is cold comfort. So is the fact that you feel satisfaction, for a while, when each accomplishment is checked off. For your relationship with the values that structure your life remains antagonistic to itself: by engaging with them in the mode of pursuit and completion, you aim at outcomes that preclude the possibility of such engagement. In pursuing a goal, you are trying to exhaust your interaction with something good, as if you were to make friends for the sake of saying goodbye. It is this structural absurdity that we learn from Schopenhauer, even if he is wrong about the agony of desire.

Following the precedent of the previous chapters, we will tread the path of spiritual progress through neologism. Begin with the activities that make up your life: getting a job, filing reports, driving home from work, listening to music, going for a walk. Borrowing jargon from linguistics, we can say that some activities are "telic": they aim at terminal states, at which they are finished and thus exhausted.[7] ("Telic" comes from the Greek "*telos*" or end, the root of "teleology.") Driving home is telic: it is done when you get home. So are projects like getting married or writing a book. These are things you can complete. Other activities are "atelic": they do not aim at a point of termination or exhaustion, a final state in which they have been achieved. As well as walking from A to B, you can go for a walk with no particular destination. That is an atelic activity. So is listening to music, hanging out with friends or family, or thinking about midlife. You can stop doing these things, and you eventually will. But you cannot complete them. They have no limit, no outcome whose achievement exhausts them and therefore brings them to an end.

Aristotle made the same distinction in his *Metaphysics*. For Aristotle, there are two kinds of "*praxis*" or action. Some are "incomplete," such as learning or building something, since "if you are learning, you have not at the same time learned." And there is "that sort of action to which its completion belongs," such as seeing, understanding, or thinking.[8] Aristotle calls activity of the first kind "*kinêsis*": it is essentially telic, aiming at its own conclusion. The upshot is that, in the apt words of philosopher Aryeh Kosman, "[its] being is autosubversive, for its whole purpose and project is one of self-annihilation."[9]

That is the problem with being consumed by plans, obsessed with getting things done. If your sources of meaning are overwhelmingly telic then whatever their value—final, existential, ameliorative—they are schemes for which success can only mean cessation. It is as if you are striving to eradicate meaning from your life, saved only by the fact that there is too much of it or that you keep on finding more. This is what Schopenhauer got right: if you focus on telic activities, your efforts work against you. Your motivation "springs from lack, from deficiency," if not from pain: the deficiency that consists in being at a distance from the terminal state at which you aim.[10] Yet in achieving that aim, you end an activity that made your life worthwhile.

It is this engine of self-destruction that powers my midlife crisis and perhaps a part of yours. I have spent four decades acquiring a taste and aptitude for the telic, for achievement and the next big thing, for personal and professional success—only to feel the void within. Fulfillment lies always in the future or the past. That is no way to live.

Social historians will ask how the ideology of striving and success developed over time, how it is historically and geographically local, how it relates to "the Protestant ethic and the spirit of capitalism" (to quote the landmark 1905 book by sociologist Max Weber).[11] We will ask, instead, how it relates to middle age. In principle, anyone could sense the emptiness at the heart of the telic orientation. A prodigy like Mill might have his crisis in advance. But it is around midlife that one's dependence on telic activities is most liable to emerge, as long-sought aims are accomplished or prove impossible. You have the job you worked for many years to get, the partner you hoped to meet, the family you meant to start—or else you don't. Until this point, you may have had no reason to reflect on the exhaustion of your ambitions and the extent to which your life is built around them. Now it becomes clear. You can feel, perhaps obscurely, the self-destructive tenor of your soul. Welcome to my world.

From this point, paths diverge. If your crisis is acute, you will see a fracture in the narrative of life: things fall apart. In Rachel Cusk's elusive novel, *Outline*, a creative writer travels to Athens to teach for the summer. Her studious reserve about her own life draws confessions from others. Here is her friend, Paniotis, telling the story of his divorce:

> In his marriage, he now realized, the principle of progress was always at work, in the acquiring of houses, possessions, cars, the drive towards higher social status, more travel, a wider circle of friends, even the production of children felt like an obligatory calling-point on the mad journey; and it was inevitable, he now saw, that once there were no more things to add or improve on, no more goals to achieve or stages to pass through, the journey would seem to have run its course, and he and his wife would be beset by a great sense of futility and by the feeling of some malady, which was really only the feeling of stillness after a life of too much motion, such as sailors experience when they walk

on dry land after too long at sea, but which to both of them signified that they were no longer in love.[12]

For Paniotis, the telic mindset, the investment of meaning above all in projects, incrementally consumed, leads to Schopenhauer's abyss: there is nothing left to do in his relationship with his wife, and so, like a treasure hunt when the last clue is cracked, it comes to an end. The fault was present from the start, hidden in the rush from A to B: love is not a project to complete.

Relationships can fail; love can be imperfect; it can fade. Philosophy will not change this. But if the source of your frustration is a telic attitude to love, a sense of its exhaustibility, having an affair won't help. Ask yourself this: do I want to be with someone else, or do I simply crave seduction, the telic thrill of falling in love again or of getting someone into bed. I don't say you won't enjoy it; maybe you will. But it too will be exhausted. Treated as a project, the affair will come to an end, and you will be back where you began: at the limit of desire. Think of Count Vronsky, seducing Anna Karenina: "He soon felt that the realization of his longing gave him only one grain of the mountain of bliss he had anticipated. That realization showed him the eternal error men make by imagining that happiness consists in the gratification of their wishes."[13]

The misconceived affair embodies a more general misconception. Suppose, like me, you are relentlessly prospective, project-driven. Beneath the bustle of activity, you hear the hollow beat of completion and discontent, an inchoate perception of self-defeat. Something is amiss. But you can't say what. It is easy to blame your choices: the wrong relationship, the wrong profession. And so you leave your partner and change careers. There may be good reasons for doing those things, but this is not one of them. It is a confused response to a midlife crisis. Sensing a flaw in your projects, you blame their particular goals, not the fact that you are goal-fixated, and attempt to start over. So long as starting over means adopting new goals, it will at most distract you from the structural defect in your life. Keeping busy is a great diversion; but it treats the symptom not the cause.

This is how I diagnose my own midlife crisis. It is partly about regret and missing out and fear of death, but mainly a response to the self-subversion of the project-driven life. My affliction is chronic, not acute, masked by the whirl of activity: more papers to grade, meetings to organize, books to read. It is not that I take no pleasure in going for a walk or spending time with friends, not getting much of anything done. But the roots of meaning in my life are principally telic: they aim at terminal states. I am not unlike Paniotis. While my condition is less extreme, its etiology is the same. I am ruefully possessed by the telic mindset. This is what explains the sense of emptiness, of repetition and futility, in getting what I want.

I cannot say how far this applies to you, how deeply you are hooked on the lure of the telic. But I am sure it is not just me. The good news is: our problem can be solved, both in theory and—stepping outside my philosophical comfort zone—in daily practice. If I am right about this, and you share my malaise, this book could change your life.

WHAT SCHOPENHAUER GOT WRONG

Love is not a project. But other things are; and some of them surely matter. It would be callous to deny the ameliorative value of curing a disease or ending a war. It would be shallow to deny the existential value of art: of reading a novel, painting a picture, singing a song. These are all telic activities; and they are all worthwhile. We should not pretend otherwise. Nor should we doubt that they have final value: they are not just means to further ends.

Does that mean we are trapped in the telic mindset? No, though it has a powerful grip on philosophy. Recent thinkers have struggled to see any alternative to a life that is centered on projects. In an influential essay, Bernard Williams, the philosopher who was bored by immortality in chapter 5, simply assumes a telic orientation: "an individual person has a set of desires, concerns or, as I shall call them, projects, which help to constitute a character"; these "ground projects [provide] the motive force which propels him into the future, and gives him a reason for living."[14] The choice of terminology is far from innocent. Not all concerns are projects, as we learned from Paniotis: there is a difference between loving someone and loving what you can do together. If only projects give us reason to live, as Williams suggests, what I have described as a midlife crisis is simply the human condition.

But Williams is wrong. You are not what you plan to get done. And the activities you love need not be projects. Atelic activities, ones that do not aim at terminal states, have value, too. There is pleasure in going for a walk, just wandering or hiking, not to get anywhere, but for the sake of walking itself. Walking is atelic: unlike walking home, it does not aim at its own completion, a point at which there is no more to do.

Advising you to go for a walk may seem a rather lame response to the angst of your midlife crisis. While it probably won't hurt, it is not the revelation you sought. You can't build your life around walking, as you might build it around the narrative of your career, your relationships, your children. But atelic activities correspond to each of the projects that structure your life. Take me, writing this book. In doing so, I am writing and thinking about philosophy: an atelic activity. This matters, I think, not just as part of finishing the book, but in its own right. If the project of writing the book gives meaning to my life, why not the non-project of doing philosophy, which has no end? If my problem is an excessive investment in telic activities, the solution is to love their atelic counterparts, to find meaning in the process, not the project. If your problem is mine, this solution will work for you.

Because they do not aim at terminal states, atelic activities are not exhaustible. Your involvement with them docs not destroy them: it does not threaten their existence, as engaging with a project does; they are not self-annihilating. This inexhaustibility has another side, expressed by Aristotle when he calls *kinêsis* "incomplete" and heralds the "completeness" of seeing, understanding, and thinking: "at the same time, one is seeing and has seen, is understanding and has understood, is thinking and has thought."[15] Atelic activities are fully realized in the present, not directed to a future in which they are archived in the past. If you want to walk home and you are not yet there, your action is incomplete, its fulfillment still to come. When you get there, it is all over. If you value going for a walk, by contrast, then in wandering through the park, you have exactly what you want. There is no more to going for a walk that what you are doing right now. You are not on the way to achieving a goal. You are already there.

That is how it is when I value writing and thinking about philosophy, not simply writing this book. What I care about is fully present, not deferred; there is no sense of emptiness or self-defeat. The same reversal can be made with activities less pretentious than philosophy. When you cook dinner for your kids, help them finish their homework, and put them to bed—telic activities through and through—you engage in the atelic activity of parenting. Unlike dinner and homework, parenting is complete at every instant; it is a process, not a project.

Try it yourself: a shift in focus from telic activities to their atelic counterparts. In general, where a project gives meaning to your life, it is possible to find meaning in the process. That meaning is not used up or consumed; it is not invested in the future but redeemed in the present.

Paniotis almost sees this, recounting an unplanned swim with his children after the divorce:

> ". . . How cold the water was, and how incredibly deep and refreshing and clear—we drifted around and around, with the sun on our faces and our bodies hanging there like three white roots beneath the water. I can see us there still," he said, "for those were moments so intense that in a way we will be living them always while other things are completely forgotten. Yet there is no particular story attached to them," he said, "despite their place in the story I have just told you. That time spent swimming in the pool beneath the waterfall belongs nowhere: it is part of no sequence of events, it is only itself, in a way that nothing in our life before as a family was ever itself, because it was always leading to the next thing and the next, was always contributing to our story of who we were. Once Chrysta and I divorced, things did not join up in that way any more, although I tried for years to make it seem as though they did. But there was no sequel to that time in the pool, nor ever will be. . . ."[16]

Swimming in the waterfall, Paniotis lives finally and fully in the present. What he does not see is that living in the present is not a suspension of ordinary life but a way of being immersed in it. Atelic activities do not occupy some rarefied peak to which we seldom ascend. If you look for them, you can find them, and find meaning in them, all around.

Neglect of this can lend a false allure to early retirement, quitting work in middle age to take up gardening or golf. I'm not saying it's a bad idea, but it is a mistake to regard such evidently cyclic and interminable pursuits as the special province of the atelic. It is there in the most stressfully purposive life, propelled from task to task. Working hard is an atelic activity, inexhaustibly present; and where completion has value, engagement has value, too. By all means quit your job, but not for the wrong reasons. There is nothing inherently telic about work.

If the sudden resignation and the wild affair do not subvert the telic orientation—if such popular tokens of the midlife crisis miss that particular point—we should turn with appreciation to a third great stereotype: buying a motorbike or sports car. The appeal of doing so has many sides, but one of them is a switch in focus from the value of getting there to the value of being on the way. One does not buy a fast car in order to arrive at one's destination more rapidly. It's about the journey; and the journey is atelic.

This is what Schopenhauer got wrong. Even if we are bound to pursue telic ends, even if they are objects of desire, they are not the only things that matter; other activities can give meaning to our lives. We can escape the self-destructive cycle of pursuit, resolution, and renewal, of attainments archived or unachieved. The way out is to find sufficient value in atelic activities, activities that have no point of conclusion or limit, ones whose fulfillment lies in the moment of action itself. To draw meaning from such activities is to live in the present—at least in one sense of that loaded phrase—and so to free oneself from the tyranny of projects that plateaus around midlife.

Where does this leave us? Knowing what we need to do but not necessarily how to do it. The transition from a telic to an atelic orientation is not routine. It is one thing to describe the atelic counterparts of telic activities, another to make the affective, emotional shift to valuing them for their own sakes, not just as means to getting things done. This is the challenge in my own life. I *want* to care as much or more about the process of writing and thinking about philosophy as I do about writing this book. But when I am working on the book, my focus is drawn to the discrete and incremental steps by which it will have to be written. I get interested in a writing problem, how to fix an argument or end a section, an article I ought to read. Absorption in projects threatens to obscure the beauty of the process, "[as] the hand held before the eye conceals the greatest mountain."[17] And so I fall into old habits, old patterns of valuation, and a familiar emptiness whose antidote I know intellectually but do not fathom in the depths of my soul.

I will not abandon you here, as I did in chapter 5, without a map. In the final section of this chapter, I relate the version of "living in the present" that emerges from our encounter with Schopenhauer to alternative visions of "mindfulness" in Buddhism and clinical psychology. I am not an expert on either, but with humility, I will chart a path between the esoteric and mundane. Mindfulness meditation has a philosophical point: something more than therapy for the stress of daily life, something less than metaphysical revelation. In finding this point, we will gain a more astute perspective on a self-help slogan and one way to put it into practice.

WHAT I KNOW FOR SURE

If there is a resonance between Schopenhauer's thought and the more hopeful teachings of early Indian philosophy, that is no coincidence. Arthur was reading Hindu scriptures in the years before he wrote *The World as Will and Representation*.[18] He studied Buddhism in the aftermath and would later call himself a Buddhist, owning a bronze statue of the Buddha that occupied a console in the corner of his apartment in Frankfurt, lit up by the morning sun.[19]

The *Bhagavad Gita*, a dialogue between warrior-prince Arjuna and his divine charioteer, Lord Krishna, which Schopenhauer read some time in 1813 or 1814, offers what is arguably a radical exhortation to the atelic attitude: "motive should never be in the fruits of action, / nor should you cling to inaction. / Abiding in yoga, engage in actions! / Let go of clinging, and let fulfillment / and frustration be the same."[20] On one reading, the counsel is to give no value at all to telic activities, to be indifferent to success in getting things done, to care only about the process, not the project. That is a harder line than my advice to value the atelic without denying that the outcome matters.

If Schopenhauer read the passage this way, it does not seem to have forestalled his pessimism, which has more in common with the Buddhism of the Four Noble Truths: life is suffering; the source of suffering is attachment; the goal is to give it up; and the way to do so is the Eightfold Path. Arthur was on board with the first two truths, shaky on the third, not so good with number four. But it is in the fourth noble truth that we find the origins of mindfulness, the idea of a way toward the end of suffering that works through meditation on the present. How similar is this idea to the ones developed above?

The answer to that question is mixed. There is a huge amount to learn from the Buddhist tradition, some of it applicable here. But there are aspects of Buddhism harder to assimilate or subtract, beginning with an abstract diagnosis of the human condition, of the sources of attachment and human suffering, that I don't accept. The contrast surfaces as soon as we move past my six-word paraphrase of the second noble truth, where "attachment" is shorthand for three things: desire, aversion, and ignorance. You can see how the first two might involve attachment, either to people and their persistence or to goals that one pursues; and you can see how detachment might help. What about the third? The traditional Buddhist view is that ignorance is key: the fundamental source of suffering is a failure to absorb the revolutionary metaphysics of *"anattā"* or no-self.[21] It is the sustained delusion of one's own enduring substance that feeds aversion and desire. Meditation for serenity (*"samatha"*) is carefully distinguished from meditation for insight (*"vipassana"*): that I do not exist is the insight that brings suffering to an end.[22]

There are stages to the meditative process, which begins with quiet, seated concentration on the breath—breathing in and out—felt calmly, almost musically in the chest or throat or nose. There is awareness of bodily sensations, sounds, suspended and detached from the need for active response. There is awareness of one's passing thoughts and feelings, equally suspended, equally detached, their ebb and flow, transient and separable. And there is, in a certain phase of meditation, an intuitive, not merely intellective grasp of impermanence, suffering, and no-self: I do not exist.[23] This is Buddhist enlightenment.

If you are perplexed by this narrative, you are not alone. You likely have questions. How can I conclude that I don't exist? Whose conclusion would that be? In pressing these questions, we echo seventeenth-century French polymath René Descartes, in one of the founding texts of modern philosophy: *cogito, ergo sum*—I think, therefore I am. Descartes argued that, since he could doubt the existence of his body and the whole material world, but not his own existence, he must be a purely immaterial substance, "the ghost in the machine."[24] But the no-self view is not just scorn for the Cartesian doctrine of immaterial souls. It finds a more profound mistake in Descartes's aphorism: the assumption that experiences, thoughts, and feelings are properties of anything at all. Instead, they are events, occurrences in a stream of consciousness, akin to flashes of light or eruptions of noise. In the century after Descartes, Georg Lichtenberg, a professor of experimental physics in Germany, complained that his argument was too quick: "We should say *it thinks*, just as we say *it lightens*. To say *cogito* is already to say too much."[25] That is the essence of the no-self view. Mental phenomena are not attributes that inhere in an object, like shape or size, but episodes in their own right.

Don't worry if you are still not sure exactly what this means. Whether the no-self view is even intelligible is one of the principal disputes about it. Not for nothing are we told that true comprehension of the insight *I do not exist* is accessible only through sustained and arduous meditation! My opinion is that that the no-self view is not intelligible. Its origin lies in a misconception shared with Descartes, that my nature, what I am, must be revealed to me in consciousness, so that if I am not a mental substance, as Descartes thought, I cannot be anything at all. Against this, I take the rather boring view that you and I are human beings and that our mental lives belong to the animals we are. That we are creatures of this kind is not something we should hope to learn by introspection.

At the same time, when I try to wrap my mind around the no-self view, I can see why Buddhists believe that it is life-transforming. If I do not exist in anything like the way that I supposed, the meaning of death is utterly changed. I will not cease to exist, after all. Instead, I have to face the fact that I was never there. To accept that fact is to let go of myself, to grieve in advance, relinquishing attachment. A similar change might undermine self-obsession—how can it survive the absence of a self?—and thus transform the character of desire.

None of this is incidental. It is the heart of Buddhist philosophy: its pivotal response to human suffering. There may be room for Buddhism without miracles, without *karma*, without the prospect of rebirth that is meant to follow from *anattā*. But Buddhism without metaphysics is like *Hamlet* without the Prince or midlife without the crisis. It is simply not the same.

Even popular adaptations of Buddhist thought have been committed to the no-self view. Alan Watts, who brought Buddhism to the Bay Area in the 1950s, was suitably unflinching: "It is convention alone which persuades me that I am simply this body bounded by a skin in space, and by birth and death in time."[26] "Never at any time are you aware of anything which is *not* experience, not a thought or feeling, but instead an experiencer, thinker, or feeler. If this is so, what makes us think that any such thing exists?"[27]

Later authors may be more evasive, but they offer no real alternative. In *Buddhism without Beliefs*, an acclaimed manifesto of secular Buddhism, Stephen Batchelor gives up on *karma* and tries to domesticate the no-self view: "The self may not be something, but neither is it nothing. It is simply ungraspable, unfindable."[28]

> The denial of "self" challenges only the notion of a static self independent of body and mind—not the ordinary sense of oneself as a person distinct from everyone else. This notion of a static self is the primary obstruction to the realization of our unique potential as an individual being. By dissolving this fiction through a centered vision of the transiency, ambiguity, and contingency of experience, we are freed to create ourself anew.[29]

The problem is that it does not take more than the ordinary sense of oneself as a person distinct from everyone else to generate attachment, selfishness, and fear of death. It is precisely because it threatens this ordinary sense—not some fiction of a static, independent soul—that the no-self view is revolutionary.

Although I reject the no-self view, my intention here is not to argue against it, but to differentiate the Buddhist conception of mindfulness from my own. The task is to say what is left of mindfulness meditation when we rescind the promise of metaphysics, a vision of transience and the nonexistence of the self.

One answer is: not insight, but serenity. We can strive to be mindful of what we are doing in order to break the chains of habit, the automaticity that prevents us from living life to the full. Attention to the present may rejuvenate us, as it did the elderly subjects of ground-breaking research by social psychologist, Ellen Langer.[30] We can meditate on breathing, on ambient noise, on our present sensations, in order to reduce our heart rates, our blood pressure, and our levels of anxiety and stress. Mindfulness-based stress reduction is now a popular tool of clinical psychology, pioneered by Jon Kabat-Zinn.[31]

These are important developments in the therapeutic use of mindfulness meditation. They treat meditation not as a path to metaphysical insight, a way to inhabit the no-self view, but as a wellspring of vitality and composure. No doubt it can play this role. But there is more to the practice of mindfulness: there is insight to be gleaned, though not the insight that you don't exist. Meditation fosters an intuitive, not merely intellective grasp of the meaning and value of atelic activities.

At the risk of embarrassment, let me admit how close we are coming to the wisdom of Eckhart Tolle, Oprah Winfrey's spiritual guru, in his 1997 blockbuster, *The Power of Now*:

If there is no joy, ease, or lightness in what you are doing, it does not necessarily mean that you need

> to change *what* you are doing. It may be sufficient
> to change the *how.* "How" is always more important
> than "what." See if you can give much more atten-
> tion to the *doing* than to the result that you want to
> achieve through it. Give your fullest attention to
> whatever the moment presents. This implies that
> you also completely accept what *is,* because you
> cannot give your full attention to something and
> at the same time resist it.[32]

Yes to the "how": to the value of doing, not just what you
aim to get done. Yes to the practice of attending to the
atelic, to the process of engagement as such. But no to
the overreach implicit in that final sentence. Tolle treats
living in the present as a panacea, a cure for every ill: "In
the Now, in the absence of time, all your problems dis-
solve. . . . You cannot be both unhappy *and* fully present
in the Now."[33] If only it were true—if it did not matter
what the present holds, only that you be open to it. But
that is wishful thinking.

Here is Sisyphus, condemned by the gods to roll a
stone to the top of a hill, only to see it roll back down
to the bottom, again and again and again for all eternity. Albert Camus wrote, in *The Myth of Sisyphus,* "[one]
must imagine Sisyphus happy."[34] Philosopher Susan
Wolf, who writes about meaning and morality, struggles
with this advice. How could Sisyphus be happy, she
complains, except by a delusion that makes him "see
something in stone-rolling that isn't really there" or by a

loss of "intelligence and . . . imaginative capacity" that impairs "his ability to perceive the dullness and futility of his labors?"[35] No measure of attention to the present should conceal the fact that a life of pointless and repetitive industry is not ideal. It is not what we want for our loved ones or ourselves. If this is how you are compelled to live, better to enjoy it than otherwise. But there are more meaningful activities to choose, ones that have ameliorative or existential worth. Philosophers may wrestle with these ideas, with the objectivity of value and our knowledge of it. Those are topics for another day. The point I am making here is that it is not sufficient for meaning in life that one attend to the present, to the atelic activities in which you are engaged. It matters what you are doing, not just that you are doing it in the Now.

Meditating on your breath, your body, the sounds in your environment is a way to train your appreciation of simple atelic activities: breathing, sitting, listening. There is value in these activities, though not enough for a meaningful life. Attending to their presence is not an end in itself. It is a way to develop your capacity to be in the moment, so as to appreciate the atelic counterparts of the telic activities that matter to you. In order to do this, you must overcome the magnetic pull of the telic orientation. You must prevent your attention from being absorbed by projects. You need the mastery of mental focus, of your own thoughts and feelings, that is nurtured by mindfulness meditation. Whether this will help in facing death, in giving up attachment to yourself, I do not know. But you can meditate for insight, if not into the no-self view, into the value of the atelic. This insight will transform your life, filling the void in the pursuit of goals, reversing the emptiness and self-destruction of the telic mindset. To live mindfully is to perceive the value of atelic activities, a value that is not exhausted by engagement or deferred to the future, but realized here and now. It is to resolve your midlife crisis, your sense of repetition and futility, of dislocation and self-defeat, by living in the halo of the present.

CONCLUSION

If you are at all like me, midlife means your memory is not what it was. Time for a brief refresher. Six chapters, eleven and a half ideas for managing middle age.

In the hollow of the U-curve, life can seem oppressive, arduous, bleak. Chapter 2 proposed two rules of midlife crisis prevention. First, as we learned from the paradox of egoism: you mustn't be too self-involved. The obsessive pursuit of happiness interferes with its own achievement: "Those only are happy," Mill wrote, "who have their minds fixed on some object other than their own happiness; on the happiness of others, on the improvement of mankind, even on some art or pursuit, followed not as a means, but as itself an ideal end. Aiming thus at something else, they find happiness by the way."[1] Second, you should make room in your life for existential as well as ameliorative value, for activities that do not answer needs we would be better off without, but make life positively good. These range from the trivial—playing games with friends—to the profundities of art and science.

Even if things go well, midlife is missing out. You recognize the paths you will never walk, the lives you will never lead, and look back with nostalgia at the liberty of youth. Some words of advice, set out in chapter 3. First, while the feeling of loss around midlife is real, ask yourself what the alternative would be. Missing out is a consequence of the plurality of values: only a drastic impoverishment in the world, or your response to it, could shield you from dismay. Second, do not overestimate the value of having options. Options matter, but not enough to compensate for outcomes you would not prefer, considered alone. Don't be fooled by the allure of choice, like Paul O'Rourke and the Underground Man. Third, while it makes sense to envy your younger self, free from the pain of missing out, do not forget the cost. Not knowing what you will not do entails not knowing what you will, a vertiginous loss of identity.

This advice falls flat when you regret what you have done or what has happened to you, when you wish you had a second chance. But as we learned in chapter 4, there are ways to reconcile yourself, without illusion, to the failings of the past. First, there is new life. Where those you love would not exist except for your mistakes, you have reason to be glad that those mistakes were made. Second, there is risk aversion. When you imagine starting over, keep in mind the many ways things could have gone, the vast uncertainty, weighed against the history you know. Is it worth the counterfactual risk? Third, there is attachment to particulars: the intricate fabric of what matters in your life. It is this plenitude you should place beside the abstract verdict that things could have gone better.

If midlife is a time to reckon with the past, it is also time to face the limits of the future. You have reached "the crest of the hill, and there stretching ahead is the downward slope with the end of the road in sight."[2] Chapter 5 took on the finitude of human life with philosophical tools. First, there is the attitude of temporal neutrality: giving equal weight to past and future gains. If you adopt this view, the deprivations of being dead are no worse than those of being as yet unconceived. Second, to want the benefits of immortality is to want what lies beyond the human condition. It is like wanting the ability to fly: a power it makes sense to envy but whose absence you should not mourn. What is left is attachment to yourself: a recognition of worth and the wish that it be preserved. Thus, half a notion for approaching middle age. Can you separate attachment from concern, grieving your own mortality in advance, giving up the need to persist forever, while saving the desire for a better life?

The most elusive challenge of midlife is not to cope with the past or the future, but with the emptiness of the present, the sense that satisfaction is deferred or left behind, that one's relentless striving is self-destructive. Our final chapter traced this malady to a structural flaw in the pursuit of projects. Projects are telic: they aim at terminal states. To engage with them successfully is to complete them and so to eliminate meaning from your life. The solution framed in chapter 6 is to invest more fully in atelic activities, ones that have no point of termination or exhaustion—activities like going for a walk, spending time with friends, appreciating art or nature, parenting, or working hard. There may not be a change in what you do from day to day. It is enough to adjust your attitude, what you love: to value not just projects but the process of raising kids, maintaining friendships, doing your job. From the outside, things might look the same; but they are profoundly different. If you value the process, you have what you want right now; and your engagement does not drain its worth. One thing we learn from the practice of meditation is how to attend to the present: to appreciate the value of the atelic amidst the glittering attraction of achievable goals. This is mindfulness at work.

It is an irony in a self-help book that its first rule is to care about things other than yourself. By all means read the book, but do it out of interest in the temporality of life, not to improve your own! According to the paradox of egoism, this irony afflicts the very enterprise of self-help, which exploits a motive that obstructs its goal. It is easy to mistrust the self-obsession and self-interest that inform the whole affair. At times, I feel that way about this book. How self-indulgent is the midlife crisis, a hardship it is a luxury to live through?

Less than we might fear. The issues I have addressed apply to almost anyone, not just a privileged few. We all face loss and limitation, roads not taken, chances missed; we make mistakes, survive misfortunes, see our efforts fail; and in the end, we die. Meanwhile, the activities that mean most to us are telic or atelic, whether we live from hand to mouth, endure oppression, or teach at MIT. In each case, your mindset can be more or less telic, goal-directed. You can focus on project after project, task after task, or value, too, the process of pursuit, whatever the projects are. Living in the present is as integral for those whose lives are tenuous or troubled as it is for anyone else.

Our quest began with Mill's impetuous dream: his plan for social reform, his vision of success, and his despair. To eradicate useless suffering is a noble aim, but it speaks to needs we would be better off without. Its value is ameliorative, not existential. There must be more to life. It is also unremittingly telic. When Mill asked how he would feel if his ambitions came to pass, he imagined a final state, a permanent utopia in which he had nothing to do. The purpose of his life had been erased.

When we strive for justice and a better world, we need the power of now as much as anywhere. To focus on the telic is to focus, all too often, on the distance and precariousness of our goals: to eradicate poverty, famine, war; to thwart the worst effects of global warming. In *Bento's Sketchbook*, his unclassifiable illustrated essay, art critic John Berger reflects on the social activism of Arundhati Roy:

> [Every] profound political protest is an appeal to a justice that is absent, and is accompanied by a hope that in the future this justice will be established; this hope, however, is not the *first* reason the

protest is being made. One protests because not to protest would be too humiliating, too diminishing, too deadly. One protests (by building a barricade, taking up arms, going on a hunger strike, linking arms, shouting, writing) in order to *save the present moment*, whatever the future holds. . . . A protest is not principally a sacrifice made for some alternative, more just future; it is an inconsequential redemption of the present. The problem is how to live time and again with the adjective *inconsequential*.[3]

There is no perfect answer to that question: consequences matter. But so do actions that abstract from them. Corresponding to a more just future, an end of telic activity, is the atelic process of protesting its absence. There is meaning in the protest.

I am still working on my midlife crisis, though I think I see the way through. I need to escape the telic mindset, to cultivate a more atelic orientation. I need to learn how to be in the moment. It's an outlook you can put to selfish use. But as it fills the emptiness of everyday life, it refuses, too, the anxiety of inconsequence in utopian schemes. It is a source of energy, focus, fullness, striving for whatever is worth striving for, to know and prize the fact that you are striving for it now.

ACKNOWLEDGMENTS

For encouragement and advice in the course of writing this book, I am grateful to Arden Ali, David James Barnett, Dylan Bianchi, Alexandre Billon, Elena Bovay, Matt Boyle, Ben Bradley, Genie Brinkema, Sarah Buss, Alex Byrne, Rachel Cohen, Earl Conee, Lorenza D'Angelo, Jason D'Cruz, Steve Darwall, Brendan de Kenessey, Cian Dorr, Kevin Dorst, Jimmy Doyle, Nicole Dular, Steve Engstrom, Jess Enoch, Kathryn Geismar, Lyndal Grant, Donald Gray, Simone Gubar, Susan Gubar, Joshua Hancox, Caspar Hare, James Harold, Sally Haslanger, Zena Hitz, Harold Hodes, Brad Inwood, Abby Jaques, Anja Jauernig, Matthias Jenny, Shelly Kagan, John Keller, Simon Keller, Michael Kessler, Jim Klagge, Hilary Kornblith, Kris McDaniel, Sam Mitchell, Dick Moran, Dan Morgan, Jessica Moss, Daniel Muñoz, Evgenia Mylonaki, Richard Neer, Philip Nel, Hille Paakkunainen, Annalisa Paese, Japa Pallikkathayil, Steve Petersen, Philip Reed, Karl Schafer, Tamar Schapiro, Sam Scheffler, Suneil Setiya, Michael Smith, Jack Spencer, Amia Srinivasan, Jason Stanley, Daniel Star, Robert Steel, Galen Strawson, Judy Thomson, Katia Vavova, Benjamin

Wald, Tom Wartenberg, Quinn White, and Leo Zaibert; and to audiences at the University of Toronto, Johns Hopkins, Union College, the University of Tennessee, the Creighton Club, Yale University, Mount Holyoke, Tulane University, the University of Pittsburgh, and MIT. Apologies to those I have forgotten.

I owe special thanks to my editor, Rob Tempio, whose enthusiasm and discernment have been crucial throughout. Brad Skow read each chapter more or less as it was written. His judicious reactions were an incentive and guide in finishing the book. Andrew Miller was the first reader of the first full draft. I am grateful for his generosity, his insight, and his sense of fact and fiction in the hypotheticals of midlife. Ian Blecher gave support when it was needed, along with wise advice about style and structure; I should have followed more of it. Sara Ellenbogen did a wonderful job of editing the text. Finally, I am grateful to the anonymous readers for the press, whose constructive comments prompted changes large and small.

And then there is Marah, who has listened indulgently, and at times impatiently, to fragment after fragment of draft after draft, whose instincts as a writer I trust implicitly, whose prose I envy, and who put up with a wealth of self-involvement while working on a book of her own. As Mill wrote of Harriet Taylor: "Her intellectual gifts do but minister to a moral character that is the noblest and best balanced I have ever met with in life." I am lucky to be sharing middle age with her. Thanks for everything, Marah. Here's to the second act.

NOTES

INTRODUCTION

1. Joseph Telushkin, *Hillel: If Not Now, When?* (New York: Schocken, 2010), 18.
2. Aaron Garrett, "Seventeenth-Century Moral Philosophy: Self-Help, Self-Knowledge, and the Devil's Mountain," *Oxford Handbook of the History of Ethics*, ed. Roger Crisp (Oxford: Oxford University Press, 2013), 230–79.

CHAPTER 1: A BRIEF HISTORY OF THE MIDLIFE CRISIS

Two books to recommend on the history and philosophy of midlife: *Middle Age* by Christopher Hamilton (Durham: Acumen, 2009), and Patricia Cohen's *In Our Prime: The Invention of Middle Age* (New York: Scribner, 2012).

1. Philip Larkin, "Annus Mirabilis," *Collected Poems*, ed. Anthony Thwaite (London: Faber & Faber, 2003), 146.
2. Elliott Jaques, "Death and the Mid-Life Crisis," *International Journal of Psychoanalysis* 46 (1965): 502–14.

3. Jaques, "Death and the Mid-Life Crisis," 506.

4. *American Beauty*, directed by Sam Mendes (Burbank: Warner Brothers, 1999).

5. John Williams, *Stoner* (New York: New York Review Books, 2003), 181.

6. Albert Camus, *The Myth of Sisyphus* (London: Penguin, 2000), 13.

7. H. G. Wells, *The History of Mr. Polly* (London: Thomas Nelson, 1910).

8. Philippe Ariès, *Western Attitudes toward Death* (Baltimore: Johns Hopkins University Press, 1974), 42–44.

9. Dante Alighieri, *Inferno*, trans. Robert Pinsky (New York: Farrar, Straus and Giroux, 1994), 3.

10. Mary Dove, *The Perfect Age of Man's Life* (Cambridge: Cambridge University Press, 1986), 28.

11. Jane Polden, *Regeneration: Journey through the Mid-Life Crisis* (London: Continuum, 2002), 7.

12. James Hollis, *The Middle Passage* (Toronto: Inner City Books, 1993), 54.

13. Edmund Bergler, *The Revolt of the Middle-Aged Man* (New York: A. A. Wyn, 1954).

14. Daniel J. Levinson, *The Seasons of a Man's Life* (New York: Ballantine, 1978).

15. Roger L. Gould, *Transformations: Growth and Change in Adult Life* (New York: Simon and Schuster, 1978).

16. Gail Sheehy, *Passages* (New York: Ballantine, 1976).

17. Erik H. Erikson, *Childhood and Society* (New York: Norton, 1950).

18. Barbara Fried, *The Middle-Age Crisis* (New York: Harper & Row, 1967), vii.

19. Joseph Heller, *Something Happened* (New York: Knopf, 1974); Doris Lessing, *The Summer before the Dark* (London: Jonathan Cape, 1973).

20. Orville G. Brim, Carol D. Ryff, and Ronald D. Kessler, "The MIDUS National Survey: An Overview," *How Healthy Are We? A National Study of Well-Being at Midlife*, ed. Orville G. Brim, Carol D. Ryff, and Ronald D. Kessler (Chicago: University of Chicago Press, 2004), 1–36, 22.

21. Brim, Ryff, and Kessler, "The MIDUS National Survey," 22.

22. Elaine Wethington, Hope Cooper, and Carolyn Homes, "Turning Points in Midlife," *Stress and Adversity over the Life Course: Trajectories and Turning Points*, ed. Ian H. Gotlib and Blair Wheaton (Cambridge: Cambridge University Press, 1997), 215–31.

23. Carolyn M. Aldwin and Michael R. Levenson, "Stress, Coping, and Health at Midlife: A Developmental Perspective," *Handbook of Midlife Development*, ed. Margie E. Lachman (New York: Wiley, 2001), 188–215, 188.

24. Jutta Heckhausen, "Adaptation and Resilience in Midlife," *Handbook of Midlife Development*, ed. Margie E. Lachman (New York: Wiley, 2001), 345–94, 345.

25. Susan K. Whitbourne, *The Search for Fulfillment* (New York: Ballantine, 2010), 160–8.

26. George Miller Beard, *American Nervousness* (New York: Putnam, 1881).

27. David Blanchflower and Andrew Oswald, "Is Well-Being U-Shaped over the Life Cycle?" *Social Science & Medicine* 66 (2008), 1733–49.

28. Terence Cheng, Nattavudh Powdthavee, and Andrew J. Oswald, "Longitudinal Evidence for a Midlife Nadir in Human Well-Being: Results from Four Data Sets," *Economic Journal*, forthcoming.

29. Alexander Weiss, James E. King, Miho Inoue-Murayama, Tetsuro Matsuzawa, and Andrew J. Oswald, "Evidence for a Midlife Crisis in Great Apes Consistent with the U-shape in Human Well-Being," *Proceedings of the National Academy of Sciences* 109 (2012), 19949–52.

30. Hannes Schwandt, "Why So Many of Us Experience a Midlife Crisis," *Harvard Business Review*, April 20, 2015, https://hbr.org/2015/04/why-so-many-of-us-experience-a-midlife-crisis.

31. Susan K. Whitbourne, Taylor R. Lewis, and Seth J. Schwartz, "Meaning in Life and Subjective Well-Being across Adult Age Groups," paper presented at the 2015 Annual Convention of the American Psychological Association.

32. Jaques, "Death and the Mid-Life Crisis," 504.

33. Richard M. Ryan and Edward L. Deci, "On Happiness and Human Potentials: A Review of Research on Hedonic and Eudaimonic Well-Being," *Annual Review of Psychology* 52 (2001), 141–66.

34. Immanuel Kant, *Critique of Pure Reason*, trans. Paul Guyer and Allen W. Wood (Cambridge: Cambridge University Press, 1998), A805/B833.

35. Aristotle, *Nicomachean Ethics*, trans. W. D. Ross and Lesley Brown (Oxford: Oxford University Press, 2009), 1100a10–1101b9.

36. Sheehy, *Passages*, 401.

37. Blanchflower and Oswald, "Is Well-Being U-Shaped?", 1741.

CHAPTER 2: IS THAT ALL THERE IS?

A readable edition of the *Nicomachean Ethics* is the Oxford World's Classics, originally translated by W. D. Ross, with revisions by Lesley Brown (Oxford: Oxford University Press, 2009). In thinking about Aristotle on finality, I have drawn on two essays by Christine Korsgaard, "Aristotle and Kant on the Source of Value" and "Two Distinctions in Goodness," both reprinted in *Creating the Kingdom of Ends* (Cambridge: Cambridge University Press, 1996), on Gavin Lawrence, "Aristotle on the Ideal Life" (*Philosophical Review* 102 [1993], 1–34), and on Gabriel Richardson Lear, *Happy Lives and the Highest Good* (Princeton: Princeton University Press, 2004). A broader introduction to Aristotle's ethics, placing him in classical context, can be found in chapter 3 of John Cooper's book, *Pursuits of Wisdom* (Princeton: Princeton University Press, 2012).

1. Jeremy Bentham, *A Fragment on Government* (Cambridge: Cambridge University Press, 1988), 3.

2. Isaiah Berlin, "John Stuart Mill and the Ends of Life," *Four Essays on Liberty* (Oxford: Oxford University Press, 1990), 175.

3. John Stuart Mill, *Autobiography* (London: Penguin, 1989), 112.

4. Mill, *Autobiography*, 145.

5. Mill, *Autobiography*, 184, 147.

6. Mill, *Autobiography*, 148.

7. Mill, *Autobiography*, 116–7.

8. Mill, *Autobiography*, 117.

9. Joseph Butler, *Five Sermons*, ed. Stephen Darwall (Indianapolis: Hackett, 1983).

10. "Beheaded Syrian Scholar Refused to Lead Isis to Hidden Palmyra Antiquities," *Guardian*, August 19, 2015.

11. Larissa MacFarquhar, *Strangers Drowning* (New York: Penguin, 2015), 189–91.

12. Jackie Robinson, *I Never Had It Made*, with Alfred Duckett (New York: Putnam, 1972), 266.

13. Aristotle, *Nicomachean Ethics*, trans. W. D. Ross and Lesley Brown (Oxford: Oxford University Press, 2009), 1094a20–22.

14. W. H. Auden, *Prose, Volume II: 1939–1948*, ed. Edward Mendelson (Princeton: Princeton University Press, 2002), 347.

15. Leo Tolstoy, "A Confession," *A Confession and Other Religious Writings*, trans. Jane Kentish (London: Penguin, 1987), 29.

16. Tolstoy, "Confession," 30.
17. Mill, *Autobiography*, 118.
18. James Anthony Froude, *Thomas Carlyle: A History of His Life in London, 1834–1881, Vol. II* (New York: Charles Scribner's Sons, 1910), 420.
19. Mill, *Autobiography*, 121.
20. Mill, *Autobiography*, 122
21. William Wordsworth, "Ode: Intimations of Immortality from Recollections of Early Childhood," *Selected Poems*, ed. Stephen Gill (London: Penguin, 2004), 157–63, 163.
22. Mill, *Autobiography*, 121.
23. Mill, *Autobiography*, 122.
24. Mill, *Autobiography*, 121.
25. Mill, *Autobiography*, 121.
26. Aristotle, *Nicomachean Ethics*, 1177b5–16.
27. Mill, *Autobiography*, 120.
28. Aristotle, *Nicomachean Ethics*, 1097a32–4, 1177b15–16.
29. Mill, *Autobiography*, 121.
30. Aristotle, *Nicomachean Ethics*, 1177b3–4.
31. Aristotle, *Nicomachean Ethics*, 1097a33–5.
32. Aristotle, *Nicomachean Ethics*, 1177b5–7.
33. Mill, *Autobiography*, 121.
34. Mill, *Autobiography*, 121.
35. Mill, *Autobiography*, 120.
36. Arthur Schopenhauer, "On the Suffering of the World," *Essays and Aphorisms*, trans. R. J. Hollingdale (London: Penguin, 1970), 41–50, 43.

37. Aristotle, *Eudemian Ethics*, trans. Anthony Kenny (Oxford: Oxford University Press, 2013), 1245a20–22.
38. Mill, *Autobiography*, 121.
39. Aristotle, *Nicomachean Ethics*, 1178b11–17.
40. Aristotle, *Nicomachean Ethics*, 1177b32–1178a2.
41. Wordsworth, "Ode: Intimations of Immortality," 158.
42. George Orwell, *Collected Essays, Journalism and Letters, Volume IV: 1945–1950*, ed. Sophia Orwell and Ian Angus (London: Mariner Books, 1971), 515.

CHAPTER 3: MISSING OUT

Philosophical accounts of incommensurability include Michael Stocker, *Plural and Conflicting Values* (Oxford: Oxford University Press, 1992) and Thomas Hurka, "Monism, Pluralism, and Rational Regret" (*Ethics* 106 [1996], 555–75), both of which inform my treatment here. (The terminology is notably inconsistent: not everyone defines "incommensurable" as I have done.) On the value of options, I credit Gerald Dworkin, "Is More Choice Better Than Less?" (*Midwest Studies in Philosophy* 7 [1982], 47–61). His essay inspired the argument I relate to Paul O'Rourke, Reggie Perrin, and the Underground Man. Besides philosophy, I recommend the novels mentioned in this chapter, including those I did not manage to discuss.

1. Richard Russo, *Straight Man* (New York: Random House, 1997); Saul Bellow, *Herzog* (New York:

Viking, 1964); Richard Yates, *Revolutionary Road* (New York: Little, Brown, 1961).

2. U.S. Bureau of Labor Statistics, http://www.bls.gov /news.release/pdf/nlsoy.pdf.

3. William Styron, *Sophie's Choice* (New York: Random House, 1979).

4. Jean-Paul Sartre, *Existentialism Is a Humanism* (New Haven: Yale University Press, 2007), 30–31.

5. Jeremy Bentham, *A Fragment on Government* (Cambridge: Cambridge University Press, 1988), 3.

6. John Stuart Mill, "Bentham," *Utilitarianism and Other Essays*, ed. Alan Ryan (London: Penguin, 1987), 132–76, 173–4.

7. Plato, *Philebus*, trans. Dorothea Frede (Indianapolis: Hackett, 1993), 21c.

8. George Steiner, *Nostalgia for the Absolute* (Toronto: House of Anansi, 2004).

9. Janet Maslin, "A Strikeout with Love and God," *New York Times*, September 16, 2014.

10. Fyodor Dostoevsky, *Notes from Underground*, trans. Constance Garnett (Indianapolis: Hackett, 2009), 11.

11. Joshua Ferris, *To Rise Again at a Decent Hour* (New York: Little, Brown, 2014), 21.

12. "Martin Amis's Big Deal Leaves Literati Fuming," *New York Times*, January 31, 1995. Amis tells the story at length in *Experience: A Memoir* (New York: Vintage, 2001).

13. Martin Amis, *The Information* (New York: Vintage, 1995), 30.

14. Nora Ephron, *I Feel Bad about My Neck* (New York: Knopf, 2008), 124.
15. Ferris, *To Rise Again at a Decent Hour*, 81.
16. Ferris, *To Rise Again at a Decent Hour*, 42.
17. Gerald Dworkin, "Is More Choice Better Than Less?" *Midwest Studies in Philosophy* 7 (1982), 47–61, 60.
18. Dostoevsky, *Notes from Underground*, 20.
19. David Nobbs, *The Death of Reginald Perrin* (London: Victor Gollancz, 1975); adapted for BBC1 as *The Fall and Rise of Reginald Perrin*, starring Leonard Rossiter.
20. Nobbs, *Death of Reginald Perrin*, 35–36.
21. Steven Wright, *I Have a Pony*, Warner Brothers B001VFM5ZG, 2009, CD.
22. Barry Schwartz, *The Paradox of Choice* (New York: HarperCollins, 2004), 125.
23. Schwartz, *Paradox of Choice*, chapter 6.
24. Meghan Daum, *The Unspeakable* (New York: Farrar, Straus and Giroux, 2014), 88.

CHAPTER 4: RETROSPECTION

I owe my appreciation of Woolf's relevance here to literary critic Andrew Miller. The quotations from Woolf's diaries appear in his lyrical essay, "The One Cake, the Only Cake" (*Michigan Quarterly Review* 51 [2012], 167–86). Readers of this book should seek it out. *The View from Here* by R. Jay Wallace (Oxford: Oxford University Press, 2013) takes a provocative, engaging look at the ethics of attachment and regret, in the wake of Robert Adams. A more detailed treatment of the views developed in this chapter can be found in my articles, "Retrospection" (*Philosophers' Imprint* 16 [2016], 1–15) and "The Ethics of Existence" (*Philosophical Perspectives* 28 [2014], 291–301).

1. Richard Ford, *The Sportswriter* (New York: Vintage, 1995), 4.
2. William Faulkner, *Requiem for a Nun* (New York: Vintage, 2012), 73.
3. R. Jay Wallace, *The View From Here: On Affirmation, Attachment, and the Limits of Regret* (Oxford: Oxford University Press, 2013), 98–99.
4. Janet Landman, *Regret: The Persistence of the Possible* (Oxford: Oxford University Press, 1993), 93–94.
5. Landman, *Regret*, 93.
6. David Foster Wallace, *The Pale King* (New York: Little, Brown, 2011), 546.
7. Hanif Kureishi, *Intimacy* (London: Faber & Faber, 1999), 4.
8. Larissa MacFarquhar, "How to Be Good," *New Yorker*, September 5, 2011, 43–53.
9. Derek Parfit, "Rights, Interests, and Possible People," *Moral Problems in Medicine*, ed. Samuel Gorovitz et al. (New York: Prentice Hall, 1976), 369–75.
10. Wallace, *View From Here*, 75–77.
11. Wallace, *View From Here*, 251, though he cites a fictional war instead.
12. James Gleick, *Chaos: Making a New Science* (London: Penguin, 1988).

13. *The Diary of Virginia Woolf, Volume 2: 1920–1924*, ed. Anne Olivier Bell (San Diego: Harcourt Brace, 1978), 221.

14. *The Diary of Virginia Woolf, Volume 3: 1925–1930*, ed. Anne Olivier Bell (San Diego: Harcourt Brace, 1980), 217.

15. Virginia Woolf, *To the Lighthouse* (San Diego: Harcourt Brace, 1981), 68–69.

16. Robert Adams, "Existence, Self-Interest, and the Problem of Evil," *Noûs* 13 (1979), 53–65, 64.

17. Plato, *Protagoras*, trans. Stanley Lombardo and Karen Bell (Indianapolis: Hackett, 1992), 358d.

18. Herbert A. Simon, "Rational Choice and the Structure of the Environment," *Psychological Review* 63 (1956), 129–38.

19. Schwartz, *Paradox of Choice*, chapter 4.

20. Immanuel Kant, *Groundwork of the Metaphysics of Morals*, trans. Mary Gregor (Cambridge: Cambridge University Press, 1998), 46–47.

21. Michael Bratman, *Intention, Plans, and Practical Reason* (Cambridge: Harvard University Press, 1987), 23–27.

22. Iris Murdoch, *The Sovereignty of Good* (New York: Routledge, 2001), 45.

23. Virginia Woolf, "Modern Fiction," *The Common Reader* (San Diego: Harcourt Brace, 1984), 146–54, 150.

24. Kureishi, *Intimacy*, 50.

25. Thomas Gray, "Ode on a Distant Prospect of Eton College," *The Complete Poems of Thomas Gray*, ed.

H. W. Starr and J. R. Hendrikson (Oxford: Oxford University Press, 1966), 10.

CHAPTER 5: SOMETHING TO LOOK FORWARD TO

I learned about the passage from Beauvoir in Susan Neiman's *Why Grow Up?* (London: Penguin, 2014), a philosophical exploration of adulthood. *How to Live* by Sarah Bakewell (London: Chatto & Windus, 2010) is a wonderful introduction to Montaigne's midlife crisis and the many answers he gave to the question it posed. On fear of death, I recommend three essays by philosophers: Thomas Nagel's "Death" (in *Mortal Questions* [Cambridge: Cambridge University Press, 1991], 1–10), Kai Draper's "Disappointment, Sadness, and Death" (*Philosophical Review* 108 [1999], 387–414) and Samuel Scheffler's "Fear, Death, and Confidence" (in *Death and the Afterlife*, ed. Niko Kolodny [Oxford: Oxford University Press, 2013], 83–110). From Draper, I take the point about immortality and excessive desire, the idea that fear of death has more than one source, and the relevance of attachment and loss. I go beyond him in drawing a connection with bereavement and the dignity of human life, and in exploring our attachment to ourselves.

1. Simone de Beauvoir, *Force of Circumstance*, trans. Richard Howard (New York, NY: Putnam, 1965), 658. I have altered the final sentence to avoid the offensive "gypped" for the French "flouée."

2. Simone de Beauvoir, *The Second Sex*, trans. H. M. Parshley (London: Jonathan Cape, 1953), 267.

3. Miranda Fricker, "Life-Story in Beauvoir's Memoirs," *Cambridge Companion to Simone de Beauvoir*, ed. Claudia Card (Cambridge: Cambridge University Press, 2003), 208–27.

4. Madeleine Gobeil, "Simone de Beauvoir: An Interview," *Paris Review* 35 (1965), 23–40, 36.

5. Gobeil, "Simone de Beauvoir: An Interview," 37.

6. Beauvoir, *Force of Circumstance*, 658.

7. Elliott Jaques, "Death and the Mid-Life Crisis," *International Journal of Psychoanalysis* 46 (1965): 502–14, 506.

8. Jaques, "Death and the Mid-Life Crisis," 506.

9. Michel de Montaigne, "To Philosophize Is to Learn How to Die," *The Complete Essays*, trans. M. A. Screech (London: Penguin, 2003), 89–108.

10. Michel de Montaigne, "On Physiognomy," *The Complete Essays*, trans. M. A. Screech (London: Penguin, 2003), 1173–1206, 1190.

11. Epicurus, "Letter to Menoeceus," *Epicurus: The Extant Remains*, trans. Cyril Bailey (Oxford: Oxford University Press, 1926), 82–93, 85.

12. Irvin D. Yalom, *Staring at the Sun: Overcoming the Terror of Death* (San Francisco: Jossey-Bass, 2008), 78–79.

13. Stephen Greenblatt, *The Swerve: How the World Became Modern* (New York: Norton, 2011), 54–55.

14. Lucretius, *On the Nature of Things*, trans. Martin Ferguson Smith (Indianapolis: Hackett, 2001), Book III: 972–7.

15. Vladimir Nabokov, *Speak, Memory: An Autobiography Revisited* (New York: Vintage, 1989), 19.

16. Nabokov, *Speak, Memory*, 19.

17. Yalom, *Staring at the Sun*, 81–82.

18. Derek Parfit, *Reasons and Persons* (Oxford: Oxford University Press, 1984), 165–6.

19. Parfit, *Reasons and Persons*, 165.

20. Anthony Brueckner and John Martin Fischer, "Why Is Death Bad?", *Philosophical Studies*, 50 (1986), 213–21.

21. Parfit, *Reasons and Persons*, 175–76.

22. Parfit, *Reasons and Persons*, 175.

23. Miguel de Unamuno, *The Tragic Sense of Life in Men and Nations*, trans. Anthony Kerrigan (Princeton: Princeton University Press, 1972), 51.

24. Bernard Williams, "The Makropulos Case: Reflections on the Tedium of Immortality," *Problems of the Self* (Cambridge: Cambridge University Press, 1973), 82–100.

25. Martha Nussbaum, "Mortal Immortals: Lucretius on Death and the Voice of Nature," *Philosophy and Phenomenological Research* 50 (1989), 303–51, 335–43; Samuel Scheffler, "Fear, Death, and Confidence," *Death and the Afterlife*, ed. Niko Kolodny (Oxford: Oxford University Press, 2013), 83–110.

26. Gobeil, "Simone de Beauvoir: An Interview," 37.

27. Stephen Mitchell, *Gilgamesh: A New English Version* (New York: Free Press, 2006), 159.

28. Philip Larkin, "Aubade," *Collected Poems*, ed. Anthony Thwaite (London: Faber & Faber, 2003), 190–91, 190.

CHAPTER 6: LIVING IN THE PRESENT

If you take one recommendation from this book, let it be the stand-up comedy of Stewart Lee, whose 2009 show *If You Prefer a Milder Comedian, Please Ask for One* (directed by Tim Kirkby [New York: Comedy Central, 2010], DVD) is a profound investigation of memory, nostalgia, and midlife. Some references may elude non-British viewers. Perhaps more approachable, but equally brilliant, is series 3 of *Stewart Lee's Comedy Vehicle* (directed by Tim Kirkby [London: Awkward Films, 2014], DVD). For Schopenhauer, try *Essays and Aphorisms*, edited by R. J. Hollingdale (London: Penguin, 1970), a selection from *Parerga and Paralipomena*. Philosophical introductions to Buddhism include Christopher Gowans's *Philosophy of the Buddha* (New York: Routledge, 2003) and Mark Siderits's *Buddhism as Philosophy* (Indianapolis: Hackett, 2007). *The Scientific Buddha* by Donald J. Lopez (New Haven: Yale University Press, 2012) is an enjoyable, wide-ranging polemic against secular appropriations of the Buddhist tradition. On the idea of a meaningful life, I recommend Susan Wolf's concise, engaging book, *Meaning in Life and Why It Matters* (Princeton: Princeton University Press, 2010). Last but not least, a good way into mindfulness is through the guided meditations offered by the UCLA Mindful Awareness Research Center, available for free on iTunes.

1. Stewart Lee, "Shilbottle," *Stewart Lee's Comedy Vehicle,* series 3, episode 1, directed by Tim Kirkby,

aired March 1, 2014, (London: Awkward Films, 2014), DVD.

2. David E. Cartwright, *Schopenhauer: A Biography* (Cambridge: Cambridge University Press, 2010), 32–33.

3. Cartwright, *Schopenhauer*, 78.

4. Cartwright, *Schopenhauer*, 88.

5. Cartwright, *Schopenhauer*, 236.

6. Arthur Schopenhauer, *The World as Will and Representation, Volume I*, trans. E. F. J. Payne (New York: Dover, 1969), 312.

7. Bernard Comrie, *Aspect* (Cambridge: Cambridge University Press, 1976), §2.2.

8. Aristotle, *Metaphysics* 9.6, 1048b18–34, as translated in Aryeh Kosman, *The Activity of Being* (Cambridge: Harvard University Press, 2013), 40.

9. Kosman, *Activity of Being*, 67.

10. Schopenhauer, *World as Will and Representation, Volume I*, 196.

11. Max Weber, *The Protestant Ethic and the Spirit of Capitalism* (London: Penguin, 2002).

12. Rachel Cusk, *Outline* (London: Vintage, 2015), 99–100.

13. Leo Tolstoy, *Anna Karenina*, trans. Louis and Aylmer Maude (Oxford: Oxford University Press, 1998), 462.

14. Bernard Williams, "Persons, Character, and Morality," *Moral Luck* (Cambridge: Cambridge University Press, 1981), 1–19, 5, 7.

15. Aristotle, *Metaphysics* 9.6, 1048b18–34, as translated in Kosman, *Activity of Being*, 40.

16. Cusk, *Outline*, 123.

17. Rabbi Nachman (1772–1810), as quoted in Martin Buber, *The Tales of Rabbi Nachman* (Amherst: Humanity Books, 1988), 35.

18. Cartwright, *Schopenhauer*, 266–69.

19. Cartwright, *Schopenhauer*, 273–74.

20. *Bhagavad Gita*, translated by Laurie L. Patton (London: Penguin, 2008), 29.

21. Donald J. Lopez, *The Scientific Buddha* (New Haven: Yale University Press, 2012), 59.

22. Lopez, *Scientific Buddha*, 84, 87.

23. Bhikkhu Bodhi, *The Noble Eightfold Path* (Onalaska: Pariyatti, 2006), 108–10; Bhante Gunaratana, *Mindfulness in Plain English* (Boston: Wisdom, 2002), 138.

24. Gilbert Ryle, *The Concept of Mind* (London: Penguin, 2000), 15.

25. Georg Lichtenberg, *The Waste Books*, ed. R. J. Hollingdale (New York: New York Review Books, 2000), Notebook K: 18, 190.

26. Alan Watts, *The Wisdom of Insecurity* (New York: Vintage, 2011), 49.

27. Watts, *Wisdom of Insecurity*, 84.

28. Stephen Batchelor, *Buddhism without Beliefs* (London: Penguin, 1998), 78–79.

29. Batchelor, *Buddhism without Beliefs*, 104.

30. Ellen J. Langer, *Mindfulness* (Boston: Da Capo, 2014).

31. Jon Kabat-Zinn, *Full Catastrophe Living* (New York: Bantam, 2013).

32. Eckhart Tolle, *The Power of Now* (Vancouver: Namaste, 1997), 67–68.

33. Tolle, *Power of Now*, 52, 62.

34. Albert Camus, *The Myth of Sisyphus* (London: Penguin, 2000), 122–23.

35. Susan Wolf, *Meaning in Life and Why It Matters* (Princeton: Princeton University Press, 2010), 23–24.

CONCLUSION

1. John Stuart Mill, *Autobiography* (London: Penguin, 1989), 117.

2. Elliott Jaques, "Death and the Mid-Life Crisis," *International Journal of Psychoanalysis* 46 (1965): 502–14, 506.

3. John Berger, *Bento's Sketchbook* (New York: Pantheon, 2011), 79–80.

INDEX